SHORT TAKES

Bite-size Taiwanese is a fun, light-hearted series helping you pick up practical, everyday Taiwanese language and interesting bits of culture through podcasts, workbooks, and more.

Bite-size Taiwanese
hello@bitesizetaiwanese.com
https://bitesizetaiwanese.com

Other Titles:
Newbie Workbook
Elementary Workbook

Available at **https://bitesizetaiwanese.com**

SHORT TAKES

A SCENE-BASED TAIWANESE VOCABULARY BUILDER

WRITTEN BY   PIN-CHIH CHI

SHORT TAKES
A SCENE-BASED TAIWANESE VOCABULARY BUILDER

Written by:	Pin-Chih Chi	紀品志	Kí Phín-tsì
Edited by:	Phil Lin	林庭逸	Lîm Tîng-ik
Designed by:	Phil Lin	林庭逸	Lîm Tîng-ik
Voice Recordings by:	Pin-Chih Chi	紀品志	Kí Phín-tsì
Audio Editing by:	Phil Lin	林庭逸	Lîm Tîng-ik

Typefaces & Fonts:
Typeset in Anton, Noto Sans TC, Noto Sans JP, Fira Sans Extra Condensed, Tāu-hū Oo (豆腐烏) published under the terms of the SIL Open Font License (OFL), Version 1.1.

Images:
Cover art by artist Rob Zs under license from Shutterstock.com.
Interior drawings by artist Rob Zs under license from Shutterstock.com and by artists Tadiga, andiz.od, and cloudstock are under license from Freepik.com.

Published by:
Bite-size Taiwanese
3F., No. 15, Sec. 1, Heping W. Rd.
Zhongzheng Dist.
Taipei City 100
Taiwan (R.O.C.)

hello@bitesizetaiwanese.com
https://bitesizetaiwanese.com

1st published: November 2020
ISBN13: 978-0-9963982-2-0 (pbk)

© 2020 BITE SIZE TAIWANESE

All rights reserved. No part of this book may be reproduced, stored in a retrieval system, or transmitted in any form or by any means (electronic, mechanical, photocopied, recorded or otherwise), without the prior written permission of the copyright holder.

TABLE OF CONTENTS

PREFACE — 6

ACKNOWLEDGEMENTS — 7

INTRODUCTION
- How to Use This Book — 8
- Conventions Used in This Book — 10
- Abbreviations — 12
- Pronunciation Basics — 13

LESSONS
- 01 It's so hot. Let's go swimming! — 24
- 02 I'm flying to the US to see my friend. — 31
- 03 He can speak English. — 38
- 04 My grandma lives in Tainan City. — 46
- 05 Let's go to the night market! — 53
- 06 Sorry, I have not been feeling well lately. — 60
- 07 Who's that lady in the picture? — 68
- 08 He bought two Christmas sweaters yesterday. — 76
- 09 It was a nice day in the morning. — 84
- 10 Your place is so far away! — 92
- 11 There are birds singing in the tree. — 101
- 12 My daughter got many gifts on her birthday. — 108
- 13 I was playing a game on my phone. — 116
- 14 Ong plays basketball every morning. — 124
- 15 These red shoes are all pretty, but... — 132
- 16 How long does it take for you to bike to the station? — 140
- 17 I was hungry in the middle of the night. — 148
- 18 There are so many mosquitoes in the house! — 157
- 19 The bathroom light was broken. — 166
- 20 Uncle always brings us a box of Swiss chocolates. — 174

ANSWER KEY — 182

INDEX — 212

PREFACE

SHORT TAKES: A Scene-based Taiwanese Vocabulary Builder lets you pick up new vocabulary in a fun, context-based way. Each lesson is based on 10 high-frequency core vocabulary words brought together in an easy-to-visualize scene, which makes learning new words simple and enjoyable.

Each core vocabulary word is presented with closely-related words, sentence patterns, common pairings, or example usages, so you'll learn the word within the broader context of the language.

Every lesson also features an imaginative short story designed to help foster a more intuitive sense of grammar, usage, and tone for core vocabulary words. Rendered in both English and natural Taiwanese sentences, the short story highlights core vocabulary words in their full native context.

Additional cultural notes related to the theme for each lesson provide even more context and background, helping you retain the new vocabulary and discover more of Taiwan's history, food, people, and society.

Writing and speaking exercises at the end of each lesson will also allow you to apply what you've learned and help review and reinforce understanding of core vocabulary.

This vocabulary builder is well-suited for self-study by beginning and elementary learners of Taiwanese.

ABOUT THE AUTHOR

Pin-Chih Chi 紀品志 **(Kí Phín-tsì)** is a linguist, translator-interpreter, language educator, and curriculum designer for Bite-size Taiwanese. He has an MA in Linguistics from Leiden University and a BSc in Agricultural Chemistry from National Taiwan University. His main languages are Taiwanese, Mandarin, English and Italian.

ACKNOWLEDGEMENTS

I am grateful to the Bite-size Taiwanese team, especially Phil Lin (林庭逸), for his support and input on this book. Since the moment I first sketched out the ideas, Phil has given me valuable feedback and suggestions. Many of our discussions have gone into the writing of this book. His design and painstaking editing work have also given the content its amazing look.

We would also like to extend our heartfelt thanks to Phînn Gān-lû (彭彥儒), Joren Pronk (蒲耀仁), and Colin Gorrie (高勝民) for reading the manuscript and giving their feedback.

Our gratitude also goes out to the countless writers, linguists, and language educators before us who have contributed to the body of Taiwanese literature, dictionaries, and resources, as well as to the software engineers who have created useful tools for the language. Their work has nurtured and benefited me in many ways, and I hope this book will benefit other teachers and learners of Taiwanese as well.

Pin-Chih Chi 紀品志 **(Kí Phín-tsì), 2020**

HOW TO USE THIS BOOK

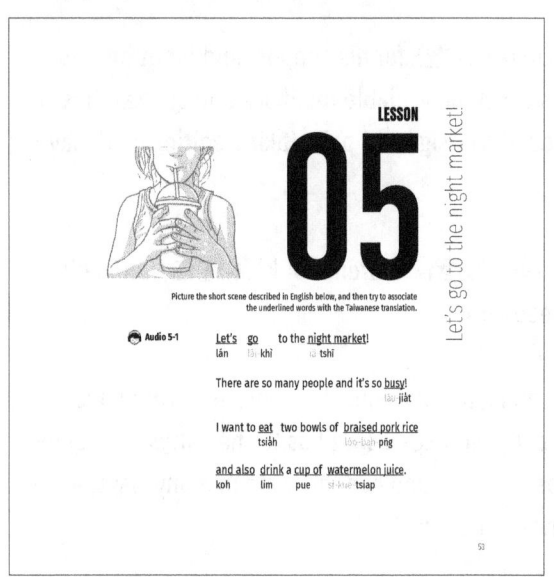

INTRODUCING THE SCENE

- Read the brief story in English first and try to picture the scene in your head.

- Listen to the audio and associate the Taiwanese word with the underlined word or phrase.

- Audio recordings available at:
  https://bitesizetaiwanese.com/shorttakes

UNDERSTANDING THE VOCABULARY

- Look at each core Taiwanese word and read the fuller explanation of its meaning.

- Expand your understanding by looking at closely related words and phrases, sentence patterns, common pairings, or example usages for each entry.

- Hear the pronunciation by listening to the audio

(Note that some related words and phrases may appear again in different lessons, but core vocabulary words are never repeated)

INTRODUCTION

NATIVE CONTEXT

- Return to the initial scene in its full native context and listen to the audio paying special attention to the core vocabulary. Then try reading it aloud yourself.

- Compare your understanding of the Taiwanese version with the English translation.

- Have even more context for the core vocabulary by getting additional cultural background.

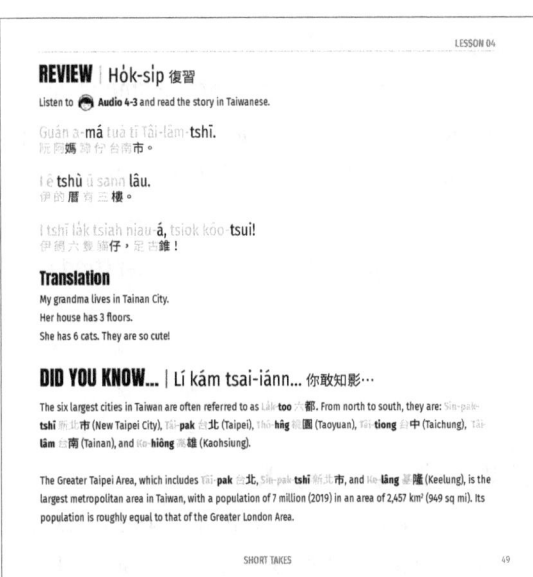

PRACTICE

- Review your understanding of the core vocabulary by completing a variety of exercises and check your responses with the **Answer Key** at the back of the book.

- Double-check your tones and tone changes (tone sandhi) against the detailed markings in the answer key.

- Test your speaking skills by forming sentences and checking your pronunciation with the audio recordings.

CONVENTIONS USED IN THIS BOOK

GENERATIONAL VARIATION

Some words or phrases are more commonly used among specific age groups. Those that have come into use more recently and tend to be used among younger speakers are marked "*new*", while those that tend to be more traditional and heard among older speakers have been marked "*trad.*".

		司哥 / 哥哥	brother (*new*)
lāu-bú 老母	mother (*trad.*)	ma-ma / ma--ma 媽媽 / 媽媽	mother (*new*)
		lāu-pē 老爸	father (*trad.*)
		pa-pa / pa--pa	father (*new*)

DIALECTAL VARIATION

While there are multiple pronunciations and variants due to the many dialects of Taiwanese, we have tried to provide the most commonly heard versions. Two of the more prominent dialects used in the media are 1) the Southern Common Dialect, which is based on the speech of Tainan and Kaohsiung, and 2) the Northern Common Dialect, which is based on the speech in Taipei.

		系按盞	
tsē / tsuē 濟	many, much, plenty	guā-tsē / luā-tsuē 偌濟	how many, how much
		tsió 少	few, little, less

Following the convention of the online dictionary by Taiwan's Ministry of Education, we list the Southern variant first, followed by the Northern variant. In some entries, there may be alternative pronunciations not splitting along the Southern/Nothern divide but instead varying because of different regional or personal preferences. In the **Index**, we have labeled **(S)** for the Southern Common Dialect and **(N)** for the Northern Commmon Dialect to show those variants that specifically differ according to this regional split.

tsē		to sit, to take (plane, bus, taxi, etc.)	2
tsē (S) / tsuē (N)	濟	many, much, plenty	2

Conventions

INTRODUCTION

JAPANESE LOAN WORDS

Many Japanese words and concepts were introduced into the Taiwanese language during the Japanese colonial period (1895-1945). Those that do not have corresponding characters are often written using Romanization. In these cases, we have also provided the original Japanese Kana in parentheses as a reference.

tsio-kóo-lè-toh (チョコレート)	chocolate	thn̂g-á 糖仔	candy
		thn̂g 糖	sugar
		piánn 餅	cookie, cracker, cake

TONE CHANGES

Tone changes on Taiwanese syllables are typically not marked in the Romanization. As a learning aid, in our book we have greyed-out all syllables requiring a tone change. Additionally, our answer key provides detailed tone change information for all Taiwanese words used in this book. For more on tones and tone changes, please read the following sections: **Tones**, p. 18 and **Tone Changes**, p. 20.

āu lé-pài 後禮拜	next week	āu-ji̍t / āu-li̍t 後日	the day after tomorrow
		āu kò gue̍h / āu kò ge̍h 後個月	next month
		lé-pài 禮拜	week; Sunday; church service
tsē hui-ki	to take a plane	tsē	to sit; to take (plane, bus

ROMANIZATION

The Romanization used in this book is Tâi-lô 台羅 which is the standard put forth by Taiwan's Ministry of Education in 2006. For more on how this corresponds to English letters and sounds, please read our brief introduction in the following section: **Pronunciation Basics**, p. 13.

CHARACTERS

Characters in this text used to represent Taiwanese are those suggested by Taiwan's Ministry of Education. Spaces between characters have also been added as an instructional aid to understand sentence structure.

ABBREVIATIONS

num	number
adj	adjective
adv	adverb
prep	preposition
verb(**-ed**)	verb ending in **-ed** (e.g. walked, jumped, etc.)
verb(**-ing**)	verb ending in **-ing** (e.g. walking, jumping, etc.)
subj.	subject (grammatical subject of sentence)
obj.	object (grammatical object of sentence)
sb	somebody
sth	something
trad.	traditional usage more often heard among older speakers
usu.	usually
lit.	literally

Indicates that audio is available at **https://bitesizetaiwanese.com/shorttakes-audio**

PRONUNCIATION BASICS

The Taiwanese syllable can be broken down into three basic elements: *initial*, *final*, and *tone*. Not all syllables have an initial, but they must have a final and tone.

INITIALS

The *initials* are consonant sounds appearing at the beginning of a syllable. Taiwanese has 17 distinct consonant sounds with some Romanized by using a combination of 2 or 3 letters (**p-**, **ph-**, **m-**, **b-**, **t-**, **th-**, **n-**, **l-**, **k-**, **kh-**, **ng-**, **g-**, **ts-**, **tsh-**, **s-**, **j-**, **h-**).

ASPIRATION

Some initials are written by combining with the letter "**-h**" (**ph-**, **th-**, **kh-**, **tsh-**). This indicates that the sound is *aspirated*, which is when a puff of air escapes from the mouth. You can feel this puff of air for yourself by placing a hand in front of your mouth as you pronounce this sound.

PALATALIZATION

Some initials, when followed by the letter "**-i**" (**tsi-**, **tshi-**, **si-**, **ji-**), become *palatalized*, which is when the placement of the tongue moves slightly backward to the *palate*, or roof of the mouth. This results in a sound that has more friction, like the sound of running water.

 Audio I-1

INITIALS (🎧)	ENGLISH APPROX.	IPA	EXAMPLES		
			TÂI-LÔ (🎧)	CHARACTER (漢字)	MEANING
p-	s**p**it	[p]	**p**it	筆	pen
ph-	**p**ie	[pʰ]	**ph**ài	派	dispatch
m-	**m**e	[m]	**m**ī	麵	noodles
b-	**b**ee	[b]	**b**í	米	rice
t-	s**t**ick	[t]	**t**ik	竹	bamboo
th-	**t**ie	[tʰ]	**th**âi	刣	to kill
n-	**n**ow	[n]	**n**áu	腦	brain
l-	**l**ie	[l] ~ [d]	**l**âi	來	to come
k-	s**k**im	[k]	**k**im	金	gold
kh-	**k**een	[kʰ]	**kh**in	輕	light
ng-	si**ng**er	[ŋ]	**ng**á	雅	elegant
g-	**gh**ee	[g]	**g**í	語	language
ts-	ca**ts**up	[ts]	**ts**ap	十	ten
tsi-	**g**in	[tɕ]	**tsi**n	真	true
tsh-	**p**izza	[tsʰ]	**tsh**á	炒	to stir-fry
tshi-	**ch**ew	[tɕʰ]	**tshi**ú	手	hand
s-	**s**igh	[s]	**s**ai	西	west
si-	**sh**ip	[ɕ]	**si**p	溼	moist
j-	ku**dz**u	[dz] / [l]	**j**û	如	if
ji-	fu**dg**y	[dʑ] / [l]	**ji**	字	character
h	**h**i	[h]	**h**ái	海	sea

FINALS

The *finals* form the core of the syllable and are typically vowel sounds.

These vowel sounds can be followed by different types of endings such as *glottal stops* (**-h**), *consonant stops* (**-p, -t, -k**), and *nasal consonants* (**-m, -n, -ng**).

In addition, Taiwanese has 2 finals that have no vowels at all, but instead are stand-alone nasal consonant endings called *syllabic nasal consonants* (**-m, -ng**).

Some vowels can also become nasalized and are marked with a double **-nn**.

 Audio I-2

FINALS	ENGLISH APPROX.	IPA	EXAMPLES			
			TÂI-LÔ	CHARACTER (漢字)	MEANING
-a	b<u>o</u>ther	[a]	b<u>â</u>	麻	numb
-e	s<u>ay</u>	[e]	s<u>é</u>	洗	to wash
-i	kn<u>ee</u>	[i]	n<u>î</u>	年	year
-o (S)	h<u>u</u>stle	[ə] / [ɤ]	h<u>ó</u>	好	good
-o (N)	h<u>o</u>	[o]	h<u>ó</u>	好	good
-oo	l<u>aw</u>	[ɔ]	l<u>ōo</u>	路	road
-u	l<u>oo</u>	[u]	l<u>ú</u>	女	female
-ai	l<u>ie</u>	[ai̯]	l<u>âi</u>	來	to come
-au	c<u>ow</u>	[au̯]	kh<u>àu</u>	哭	to cry
-ia	pap<u>aya</u>	[i̯a]	i<u>á</u>	野	wild
-io (S)	j<u>er</u>k	[i̯ə] / [i̯ɤ]	ts<u>ió</u>	少	few
-io (N)	J<u>oe</u>	[i̯o]	ts<u>ió</u>	少	few
-iu	ch<u>ew</u>	[i̯u]	tsh<u>iú</u>	手	hand
-ua	sw<u>ab</u>	[u̯a]	s<u>ua</u>	沙	sand
-ue	w<u>ay</u>	[u̯e]	u<u>ê</u>	話	speech
-ui	w<u>ee</u>	[u̯i]	u<u>ī</u>	胃	stomach
-iau	m<u>eow</u>	[i̯au̯]	n<u>iau</u>	貓	cat
-uai	wh<u>y</u>	[u̯ai̯]	u<u>ai</u>	歪	crooked

S = Southern Common Dialect
N = Northern Common Dialect

INTRODUCTION

 Audio I-3

FINALS	ENGLISH APPROX.	IPA	EXAMPLES		
			TÂI-LÔ	CHARACTER (漢字)	MEANING
-ah	B<u>ah</u>! Humbug!	[aʔ]	b<u>ah</u>	肉	flesh
-eh	<u>eh</u>	[eʔ]	<u>e̍h</u>	狹	narrow
-ih	b<u>e</u>ak	[iʔ]	b<u>ih</u>	覕	hide
-oh (S)	d<u>uh</u>	[əʔ] / [ɤʔ]	t<u>oh</u>	桌	table
-oh (N)	d<u>ough</u>	[oʔ]	t<u>oh</u>	桌	table
-ooh	<u>aw</u>estruck	[ɔʔ]	<u>ooh</u>	喔	oh!
-uh	s<u>ou</u>p	[uʔ]	s<u>uh</u>	欶	to suck in
-aih	h<u>ai</u>ku	[aiʔ]	h<u>aih</u>	唉	(sigh)
-auh	g<u>ou</u>ge	[auʔ]	k<u>auh</u>	軋	to run over
-iah	ter<u>iya</u>ki	[iaʔ]	th<u>iah</u>	拆	to rip apart
-ioh (S)	y<u>ear</u>n (with pursed lips)	[iəʔ] / [iɤʔ]	h<u>ioh</u>	歇	to rest
-ioh (N)	<u>yo</u>ke	[ioʔ]	h<u>ioh</u>	歇	to rest
-iuh	d<u>ew</u> point	[iuʔ]	t<u>iuh</u>	搐	throb
-uah	m<u>uah</u> (kiss)	[uaʔ]	kh<u>uah</u>	闊	broad
-ueh	w<u>a</u>fer	[ueʔ]	<u>ue̍h</u>	劃	to draw a line
-iauh	<u>Yow</u>zers!	[iauʔ]	h<u>iauh</u>	蹶	to warp or peel

S = Southern Common Dialect
N = Northern Common Dialect

STOPS

Stops are consonant sounds that result when the air passing through the vocal tract is blocked or "stopped".

GLOTTAL STOPS

Finals that end in **-h** indicate that there is a *glottal stop*, which is when the airflow is abruptly stopped by closing the vocal cords.

In English, this happens, for example, in between the syllables of "uh-oh".

SHORT TAKES

CONSONANT STOPS

Finals that end in *consonant stops* (**-p**, **-t**, **-k**) do not release air at the end of the sound.

In English, this is similar to what often happens to the consonant ending of the first word in a compound word, such as the "**-ck**" in "bla**ck**board", or the "**-p**" in "cu**p**cake".

NASALS

Nasals are when air escapes from the nose. Taiwanese has both nasal consonant finals (two of which can also be syllabic, meaning they require no vowel) and nasal vowels.

NASAL CONSONANT FINALS

Finals in Taiwanese can end in the *nasal consonants* (**-m, -n, -ng**). Note that the vowels that precede these endings are slightly nasalized in anticipation of saying these nasal consonant finals, but their nasalization is not as strong as on distinct nasal vowels.

 **Audio I-4**

FINALS	ENGLISH APPROX.	IPA	EXAMPLES TÂI-LÔ	CHARACTER (漢字)	MEANING
-ap	c**op** car	[ap̚]	kh**ap**	匼	to face down
-at	sp**ot**light	[at̚]	p**àt**	別	other
-ak	s**ock** puppet	[ak̚]	s**ak**	揀	to push
-ip	sh**ip**wreck	[ip̚]	s**ip**	溼	moist
-it	sp**it**ball	[it̚]	p**it**	筆	pen
-ik	k**ick**stand	[iǝk̚] / [ik̚]	kh**ik**	刻	to carve
-ok	l**ock**smith	[ɔk̚]	l**ok**	橐	sack
-ut	s**oot**-black	[ut̚]	s**ùt**	術	skill
-iap	y**up** yup!	[iap̚]	**iap**	揜	to conceal
-iat	j**et**lag	[iɛt̚]~[ɛt̚]	j**iàt**	熱	hot
-iak	y**uck** factor	[iak̚]	s**iak**	摔	to tumble
-iok	y**oke**-toed	[iɔk̚]	**iok**	約	to schedule
-uat	**what**	[uat̚]	**uat**	斡	to turn
-am	s**um**	[am]	s**àm**	搧	to slap
-an	b**on**net	[an]	b**ân**	慢	slow
-ang	g**ong**	[aŋ]	k**áng**	港	harbor
-im	d**im**	[im]	t**îm**	沉	to sunk
-in	b**een**	[in]	b**īn**	面	face
-ing	t**yi**ng	[iǝŋ] / [iŋ]	**îng**	閒	idle
-om	**om**elet	[ɔm]	**om**	掩	to conceal
-ong	**own** goal	[ɔŋ]	**ông**	王	king
-un	**Ow**en	[un]	**ūn**	運	to move
-iam	y**um**	[iam]	i**âm**	鹽	salt
-ian	y**en**	[iɛn]~[ɛn]	i**án**	演	to perform
-iang	**Yon**kers	[iaŋ]	i**ang**	央	to request
-iong	we **own** gold	[iɔŋ]	t**iong**	中	middle
-uan	q**uan**tum	[uan]	kh**uán**	款	to gather up

INTRODUCTION

 Audio I-5

FINALS	ENGLISH APPROX.	IPA	EXAMPLES		
			TÂI-LÔ	CHARACTER (漢字)	MEANING
-m	pri<u>sm</u>	[m̩]	m̄	毋	not
-ng	to<u>ng</u>ue	[ŋ̍]	th<u>ng</u>	湯	soup
-ann	n<u>o</u>nsense *(nasalized)*	[ã]	k<u>ànn</u>	敢	to dare
-enn	s<u>e</u>nsor *(nasalized)*	[ẽ]	s<u>enn</u>	生	to give birth
-inn	t<u>ee</u>n *(nasalized)*	[ĩ]	th<u>inn</u>	添	to add
-onn	<u>ow</u>ner *(nasalized)*	[õ]	<u>onn</u>	嗚	buzz
-ainn	m<u>i</u>ning *(nasalized)*	[ãĩ]	k<u>ainn</u>	唉	to cry out
-iann	hern<u>ia</u> *(nasalized)*	[ĩã]	k<u>iann</u>	驚	scared
-iunn	n<u>ew</u> *(nasalized)*	[ĩũ]	s<u>iunn</u>	箱	box
-uann	ig<u>ua</u>na *(nasalized)*	[ũã]	k<u>uânn</u>	寒	cold
-uinn	w<u>ee</u>ning *(nasalized)*	[ũĩ]	h<u>uînn</u>	橫	horizontal
-uainn	wh<u>i</u>ning *(nasalized)*	[ũãĩ]	u<u>áinn</u>	踤	to sprain
-annh	h<u>o</u>nking *(nasalized)*	[ã?]	h<u>annh</u>	熻	scald
-ennh	k<u>e</u>nnel *(nasalized)*	[ẽ?]	kh<u>ěnnh</u>	喀	*(cough)*
-onnh	h<u>o</u>mely *(nasalized)*	[õ?]	h<u>onnh</u>	乎	right?
-iannh	man<u>ia</u>cal *(nasalized)*	[ĩã?]	h<u>iannh</u>	挔	to pick up cloth

SYLLABIC NASAL CONSONANTS

There are two nasal consonant finals that are *syllabic*, meaning they do not need vowel sounds and can also be syllables on their own: **-m** or **-ng**.

NASAL VOWELS

When you pronounce a *nasal vowel*, the air not only comes out from your mouth but also escapes through your nose.

Finals that end in **-nn** indicate that the preceding vowel is nasalized.

In addition, when syllables begin with **m-**, **n-**, or **ng-**, the entire syllable, including the final, is nasalized. However, by convention the **-nn** is not written. For example, a word like "**mīnn**" [mĩ] is actually written as **mī**.

English does not have distinct nasal vowels like in Taiwanese, but in English, vowels adjacent to nasal consonants do become slightly nasalized, like the "**o**" in "n<u>o</u>nsense".

Nasal vowels can also have glottal stops and are marked as **-nnh**.

SHORT TAKES

TONES

There are two parts when talking about tone: *pitch* and *contour*.

PITCH - To help describe the *pitch* of the voice, the vocal register is generally divided into three levels: **high**, **mid**, and **low**. The *mid* pitch should be close to your normal speaking voice.

CONTOUR - The *contour* describes how that pitch might change over the duration of the syllable. In Taiwanese, there are four types: ***flat***, ***falling***, ***rising***, or ***stop***.

BASIC TONES

There are 7 basic tones in modern Taiwanese.

Tone 1 is a ***high flat*** tone and does not have a diacritic. Note that syllables without a diacritic but ending in **-p**, **-t**, **-k**, or **-h** are Tone 4.

Tone 2 is a ***high falling*** tone and marked with an acute accent (´).

Tone 3 is a ***mid falling*** tone and marked with a grave accent (`).

Tone 4 is a ***mid stop*** tone and does not have a diacritic. As a "stop" tone, the syllable ends in an unreleased **-p**, **-t**, **-k**, or **-h**.

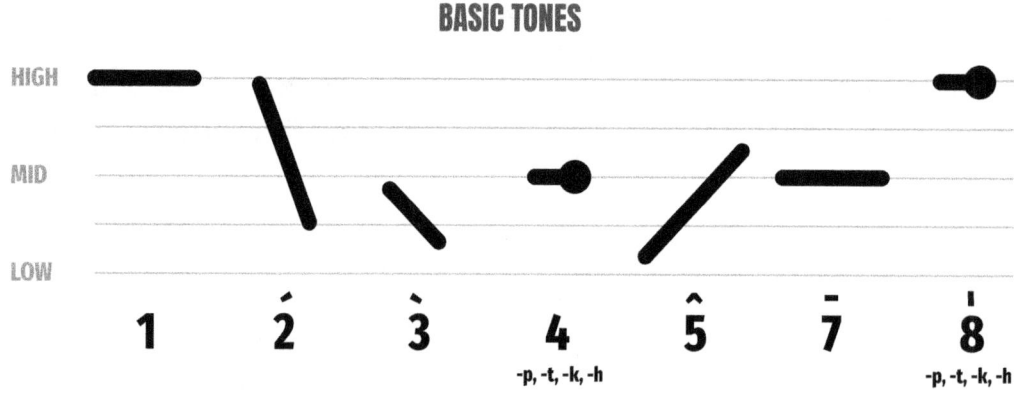

BASIC TONES

 **Audio I-6**

TONES			EXAMPLES		
NUMBER	DESCRIPTION	MARKING	TÂI-LÔ	CHARACTER (漢字)	MEANING
0	Neutral	--a	--ê	的	*gram. suffix*
1	High Flat	a	e	挨	to shove
2	High Falling	á	é	矮	short
3	Mid Falling	à	è	裔	descendant
4	Mid Stop	ah	eh	厄	disaster
5	Low Rising	â	ê	鞋	shoe
7	Mid Flat	ā	ē	下	below
8	High Stop	a̍h	e̍h	狹	narrow
9*	Mid Rising	ǎ	ǐng (e-hng)	下昏	evening

Tone 5 is a ***low rising*** tone and marked with a circumflex accent (ˆ).

Tone 6 is no longer used because it has been merged with other tones in almost all modern Taiwanese dialects.

Tone 7 is a ***mid flat*** tone and marked with a macron accent (ˉ).

Tone 8 is a ***high stop*** tone and marked with a vertical line accent (ˈ). As a "stop" tone, the syllable ends in an unreleased **-p**, **-t**, **-k**, or **-h**.

Tone 0 is a common way to refer to neutral tones, which are syllables that have lost their original tone and become shorter and lighter. This happens when a word is de-emphasized and becomes more like a grammatical particle. The de-emphasis can also result in particular word pairs that have different meanings but contrast only in the use of Tone 0. Syllables that have been neutralized are preceded by a double-hyphen (--).

* "**Tone 9**" is not an official tone but refers to a phenomenon where a contraction (**tiǒng** = **tiong-ng** 中央 "center"), triplicated adjective (**ǎng-âng-âng** 紅紅紅 "extremely red"), or loan word (**ěn-jin** = エンジン "engine") results in a ***mid rising*** tone. It is sometimes marked with a double acute accent (˝).

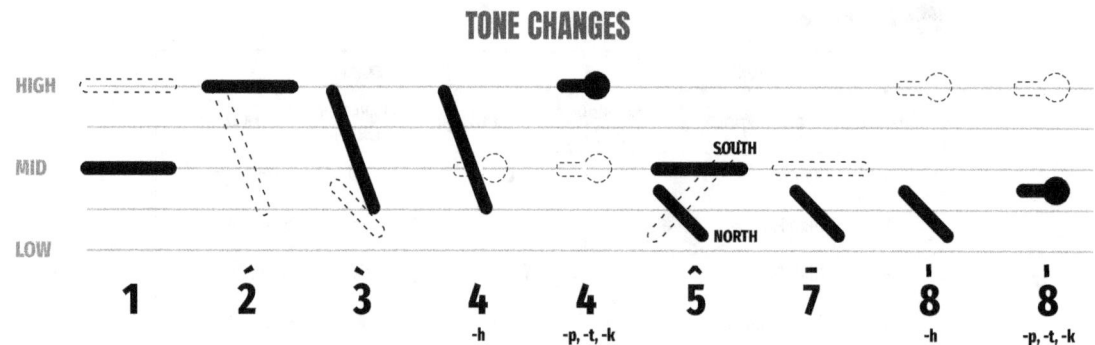

TONE CHANGES

Every syllable in Taiwanese has an original tone, sometimes called its "citation form". When a monosyllabic word is said in isolation, it is pronounced in its original tone.

When more syllables and words are combined to form a phrase or sentence, some syllables change tone to a shape similar to another tone, sometimes called the "sandhi form".

In Taiwanese, tone changes happen due to grammar and sentence structure and help with tasks like grouping ideas within a sentence, indicating parts-of-speech, showing emphasis, etc.

Although there are many rules and contexts requiring a tone change (that is beyond the scope of this book), one basic rule is that **the syllable at the end of a phrase stays in the original tone**. In other words, **all the syllables before that final syllable should change tone**, unless there's another tone change rule that supercedes it.

So, the tones on a string of words within a sentence could be like:

change-change-change-**original**, change-change-change-**original**, change-change-change-**original**.

You can think of syllables that are in their original tone as "destinations" or "resting spots" in your sentences. The syllable in the original tone and all the changed tones before it can be grouped together as a whole phrase (or a "tone sandhi group"). If you were to put commas into your sentence, those would also be the natural places to show where these phrases occur.

Pronunciation Basics

INTRODUCTION

TONE CHANGE LEARNING TIPS

Sometimes it can be difficult to remember *which* tone changes to *which* tone. Here are 3 tips to help you simplify the story and internalize how the tones change.

1) **STEP DOWN, BOUNCE UP, AND HOLD!**
2) **PUSH IT DOWN!**
3) **SWAP & DROP**

TIP 1: STEP DOWN, BOUNCE UP, AND HOLD!

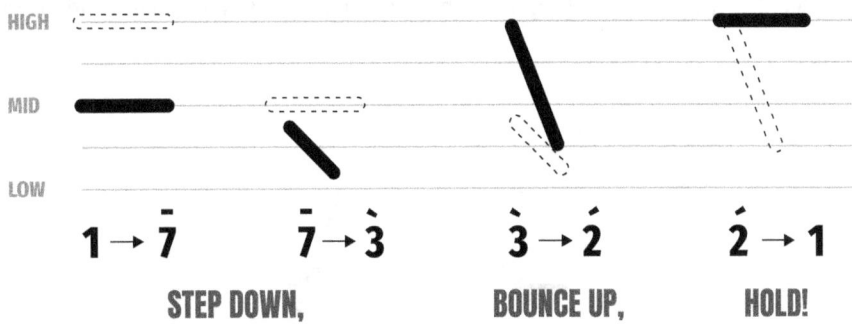

STEP DOWN: Tone 1 changes to Tone 7 (*high flat* ⇒ *mid flat*), Tone 7 changes to Tone 3 (*mid flat* ⇒ *mid falling*). Think of it like **stepping down** stairs.

BOUNCE UP: Since Tone 3 (*mid falling*) can't step down any further, **bounce up** back to the top and then begin to come down again, but this time as Tone 2 (*high falling*).

HOLD: For Tone 2 (*high falling*), begin at the same starting point high up, but instead of falling, just **hold** at the position for a Tone 1 (*high flat*).

TIP 2: PUSH IT DOWN!

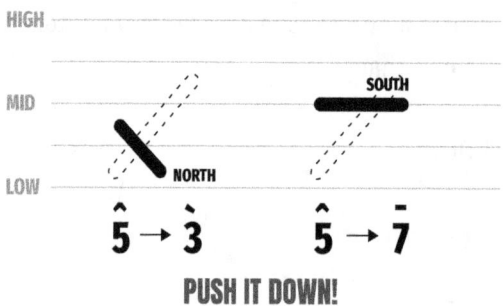

Tone 5 is originally a rising tone, but when it needs to change tone **push it down** to keep it from rising. Note that in some Northern dialects it changes to a Tone 3 (*mid falling*), while in Southern dialects, it changes to a Tone 7 (*mid flat*). You can also simplify it by imagining you don't have enough time to rise, so instead just give it a brief mid pitch.

TIP 3: SWAP & DROP

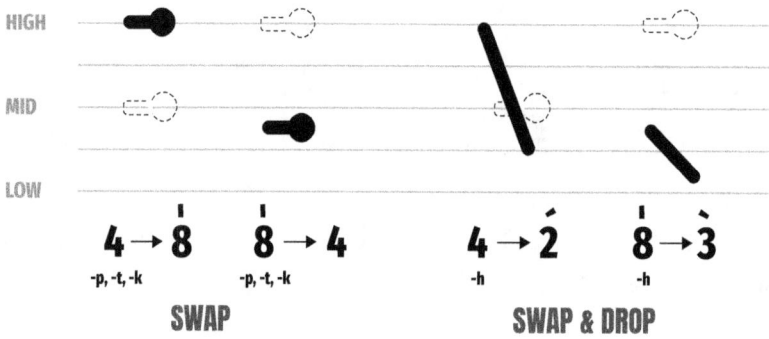

Tone 4 (*mid stop*) and Tone 8 (*high stop*) are the two "stop tones".

SWAP (for -ptk): For the stop tones ending in the **-p**, **-t**, or **-k**, Tone 4 and Tone 8, basically **swap**: *mid stop* ⇒ *high stop*, and *high stop* ⇒ *mid stop*.

SWAP & DROP (for -h): For the stop tones ending in **-h**, they not only **swap** places, but also **drop** their -h's (meaning they lose the glottal stops), and **drop** in pitch: *mid stop* ⇒ *high falling*, and *high stop* ⇒ *mid falling*.

One great way to become familiar with how a certain tone changes is to use reduplicated adjectives. In Taiwanese, reduplicating an adjective has the effect of lessening the intensity. It also works as a nice example for tone changes because you have the same syllable twice, but one in the changed tone, and the other in the original tone.

Below is a summary of the tone change rules using some reduplicated adjectives as examples:

 Audio I-7

TONE CHANGES		REDUPLICATED ADJECTIVE EXAMPLES		
ORIGINAL	CHANGED	TÂI-LÔ	CHARACTER (漢字)	MEANING
1	7	oo, oo⁷-oo	烏, 烏烏	black, a little black
2	1	nńg, nńg¹-nńg	軟, 軟軟	soft, a little soft
3	2	tshàu, tshàu²-tshàu	臭, 臭臭	stinky, a little stinky
4h	2	khuah, khuah²-khuah	闊, 闊闊	wide, a little wide
4p,t,k	8	sip, sip⁸-sip	濕, 濕濕	moist, a little moist
5 (S)	3	âng, âng⁷-âng	紅, 紅紅	red, a little red
5 (N)	7	âng, âng³-âng	紅, 紅紅	red, a little red
7	3	kāu, kāu³-kāu	厚, 厚厚	thick, a little thick
8h	3	pe̍h, pe̍h³-pe̍h	白, 白白	white, a little white
8p,t,k	4	ku̍t, ku̍t⁴-ku̍t	滑, 滑滑	slippery, a little slippery

S = Southern Common Dialect
N = Northern Common Dialect

LESSON 01

It's so hot. Let's go swimming!

Picture the short scene described in English below, and then try to associate the underlined words with the Taiwanese translation.

 Audio 1-1

It's <u>so</u> <u>hot</u> <u>today</u>.
    tsiok jua̍h kin-á-ji̍t

<u>I</u> <u>want</u> <u>to go</u> <u>swimming</u>
Guá beh khì siû-tsuí

this <u>afternoon</u>.
  e-poo

My <u>dog</u> <u>also</u> wants to go.
   káu mā

VOCABULARY | Gí-sû 語詞

 Audio 1-2

WORD	MEANING	RELATED WORDS	MEANING
tsiok / tsok 足	so, very	tsiânn 誠	really, truly, very
		tsin 真	really, truly, very
ju̍ah / lu̍ah 熱	hot (weather)	ju̍ah-thinn / lu̍ah-thinn 熱天	summer
		kuânn 寒	cold (weather)
		kuânn-thinn 寒天	winter
kin-á-ji̍t / kin-á-li̍t 今仔日	today	tsit-má 這馬	now
guá 我	I, me	guá ê 我的	my, mine
		guán / gún 阮	we, us, our (excluding listener); my
		guán ê / gún ê 阮的	our, ours (excluding listener)
		lí 你	you (singular)
		lí ê 你的	your (singular), yours

SHORT TAKES

WORD	MEANING	RELATED WORDS	MEANING
		lín 恁	you (plural); your
		lín ê 恁 的	your (plural), yours
beh / bueh 欲	to want; to be going to	siūnn-beh / siūnn-bueh 想欲	would like to; to want
khì 去	to go (to)	lâi 來	to come (to)
siû-tsuí 泅水	to swim; swimming	siû 泅	to swim
e-poo 下晡	afternoon	tsái-khí / tsá-khí 早起	morning
		àm-sî 暗時	evening
káu 狗	dog	káu-á 狗仔	dog, puppy
mā 嘛	also, too		

It's so hot. Let's go swimming!

REVIEW | Ho̍k-si̍p 復習

Listen to Audio 1-3 and read the story in Taiwanese.

Kin-á-ji̍t tsiok jua̍h!
今仔日 足 熱！

Guá e-poo beh khì siû-tsuí.
我 下晡 欲 去 泅水。

Guá ê káu mā beh khì siû.
我 的 狗 嘛 欲 去 泅。

Translation

It's so hot today.
I want to go swimming this afternoon.
My dog also wants to go.

DID YOU KNOW... | Lí kám tsai-iánn... 你敢知影...

Taiwan is a subtropical-tropical island. While the annual average temperature is a comfortable 22°C (72°F), in the summertime temperatures typically range from 25°C to 32°C (77–90°F). Quite hot, isn't it?

By contrast, the winter is mild, typically around 18°C (64°F), though occasionally there is snowfall in higher elevations near the mountaintops. Because of this, people often describe Taiwan as "**sù-kuì-jû-tshun** 四季如春", a saying that means "the four seasons are all like spring". However, don't be fooled by the seemingly high temperatures in winter. The island's high humidity and near absence of indoor heating can make even a 10°C (50°F) day feel bone-chillingly cold!

SHORT TAKES

EXERCISES | Liān-si̍p 練習

E01 Match each Taiwanese word to its English translation.

1. siû-tsuí   ____   (a) to go
2. tsiok   ____   (b) today
3. beh   ____   (c) I, me
4. khì   ____   (d) to swim
5. e-poo   ____   (e) to want
6. káu   ____   (f) dog
7. mā   ____   (g) so, very
8. jua̍h   ____   (h) hot
9. kin-á-ji̍t   ____   (i) also, too
10. guá   ____   (j) afternoon

E02 Fill in the blanks using one of the words you've learned in this lesson.

1. (_____) tsiok kuânn!
   It's so cold today!

2. Guá e-poo beh khì (_____).
   I want to go swimming this afternoon.

3. Guá ê (_____) mā beh khì siû.
   My dog also wants to go swimming.

4. Tsit-má (_____) jua̍h.
   It's so hot now.

5. Guán (_____) siūnn-beh khì.
   We would like to go, too.

E03 Can you figure out how to say...?

Take a look at the vocabulary list and see if you can figure out how to say these sentences in Taiwanese:

1. "I'm going to swim now."
2. "It was cold in the morning. It was cold in the evening, too."

Listen to 🎧 **Audio 1-4** and see how you did!

LESSON 02

I'm flying to the US to see my friend.

Picture the short scene described in English below, and then try to associate the underlined words with the Taiwanese translation.

Audio 2-1

I <u>have</u>   <u>a friend</u>   who <u>lives in</u>   <u>the US</u>.
ū   tsıt ê pîng-iú   tuà   Bí-kok

<u>Next week</u> I will <u>take a plane</u> there.
āu lé-pài   tsē hui-ki

I <u>am carrying</u> <u>a lot</u> of <u>instant ramen</u> with me!
tsah   tsē   phàu-mī

31

VOCABULARY | Gí-sû 語詞

🎧 Audio 2-2

WORD	MEANING	RELATED WORDS	MEANING
ū 有	to have, to exist	bô 無	to not have, to not exist, without; not, no
tsi̍t ê 一个	one, a	tsi̍t 一	one
		ê 个	(general *measure word*)
		num + ê + noun	
		nn̄g 兩	two
		tsiah 隻	(*measure word* for ships, airplanes and most animals)
		nn̄g tsiah káu-á 兩 隻 狗仔	two dogs
pîng-iú 朋友	friend	tshù-pinn 厝邊	neighbor; neighborhood
tuà 蹛	to live (in), to stay at	tuà tī 蹛佇	to live in, at, on
Bí-kok 美國	United States	kok 國	country
		Ing-kok 英國	United Kingdom
		Hân-kok 韓國	Korea

I'm flying to the US to see my friend.

LESSON 02

WORD	MEANING	RELATED WORDS	MEANING
		Tâi-uân 台灣	Taiwan
		Ji̍t-pún / Li̍t-pún 日本	Japan
āu lé-pài 後禮拜	next week	āu--ji̍t / āu--li̍t 後日	the day after tomorrow
		āu kò gue̍h / āu kò ge̍h 後個月	next month
		lé-pài 禮拜	week; Sunday; church service
tsē hui-ki 坐飛機	to take a plane	tsē 坐	to sit; to take (plane, bus, taxi, etc.)
		hui-ki / hue-lîng-ki 飛機 / 飛行機	plane
		hué-tshia / hé-tshia 火車	train
		kong-tshia / bah-suh 公車 / (バス)	bus
		kè-thîng-tshia / kè-tîng-tshia 計程車	taxi
tsah 紮	to bring, to carry (usu. smaller items in a pocket or bag)	tsah tsînn 紮錢	to bring/have money in one's pocket
		tsah piān-tong 紮便當	to carry a lunchbox ("bento")
tsē / tsuē 濟	many, much, plenty	guā-tsē / luā-tsuē 偌濟	how many, how much
		tsió 少	few, little, less

SHORT TAKES

WORD	MEANING	RELATED WORDS	MEANING
phàu-mī 泡麵	instant ramen	phàu 泡	to infuse in hot water; to make (tea, hot chocolate, coffee, milk, etc)
		mī 麵	noodles
		phàu tê 泡 茶	to brew tea

I'm flying to the US to see my friend.

LESSON 02

REVIEW | Ha̍k-si̍p 復習

Listen to Audio 2-3 and read the story in Taiwanese.

Guá ū tsi̍t ê pîng-iú tuà Bí-kok.
我有一個朋友蹛美國。

Guá āu lé-pài beh tsē hui-ki khì.
我後禮拜欲坐飛機去。

Guá tsah tsiok tsē phàu-mī!
我紮足濟泡麵！

Translation

I have a friend who lives in the US.

Next week I will take a plane there.

I am carrying a lot of instant ramen with me!

DID YOU KNOW... | Lí kám tsai-iánn... 你敢知影…

Many Taiwanese like to travel with instant ramen. Why? Because it's just so convenient and tastes so good! Sometimes when Taiwanese travel abroad and miss home, a cup of instant ramen can become the ultimate comfort food.

Fun fact: The inventor and "father of instant noodles", Momofuku Ando (安藤 百福), was born in 1910 as **Ngôo Pik-hok** 吳 百福 to a wealthy Taiwanese family in **Ka-gī** 嘉義 (Chiayi), Taiwan while it was still under Japanese rule. Both of his parents died young, so he was raised by his grandfather, who ran a wholesale textiles business in **Tâi-lâm** 台南 (Tainan). **Ngôo Pik-hok** 吳 百福 later started his own trade company in **Tâi-pak** 台北 (Taipei), importing fabrics from Japan. While his business grew, he traveled to Japan for study and received a degree in Economics. After the Second World War, he stayed in Japan, took his Japanese wife's surname "Ando", and founded Nissin Food Products, a Japanese food company specializing in instant noodles.

SHORT TAKES

EXERCISES | Liān-si̍p 練習

E01 Match each Taiwanese word to its English translation.

1. tuà   _____   (a) United States
2. Bí-kok   _____   (b) next week
3. tsi̍t ê   _____   (c) to take a plane
4. āu lé-pài   _____   (d) instant ramen
5. ū   _____   (e) to have, to exist
6. phàu-mī   _____   (f) to bring, to carry with oneself
7. tsē hui-ki   _____   (g) many, much, plenty
8. tsah   _____   (h) to live (in), to stay at
9. tsē   _____   (i) one, a
10. pîng-iú   _____   (j) friend

E02 Choose the right verb to complete each sentence.

1. Guá (tuà / ū / khì / tsē) nn̄g ê pîng-iú.
   I have two friends.

2. Guá tsit-má (tuà / ū / khì / tsē) tī Bí-kok.
   I'm living in the US now.

3. Guá kin-á-ji̍t beh (tuà / ū / khì / tsē) hui-ki (tuà / ū / khì / tsē) Ji̍t-pún.
   I'm taking a plane to Japan today.

E03 Translate the sentences into English.

1. Guá ū tsiok tsē pîng-iú.

   _____.

2. Lí ê pîng-iú āu lé-pài beh khì Bí-kok.

   _____.

3. Guá ū tsah tsînn.

   _____.

4. Lí ū guā-tsē phàu-mī?

   _____.

E04 Can you figure out how to say…?

Take a look at the vocabulary list and see if you can figure out how to say these sentences in Taiwanese:

1. "I have two dogs."
2. "I have no friends."
3. "I live in the UK."

Listen to **Audio 2-4** and see how you did!

SHORT TAKES

LESSON 03

He can speak English.

Picture the short scene described in English below, and then try to associate the underlined words with the Taiwanese translation.

 Audio 3-1

<u>He</u> <u>can</u> <u>speak</u> <u>English</u>.
i   ē-hiáu kóng   Ing-gí

<u>His</u> <u>girlfriend</u> <u>is</u> <u>British</u>.
lú pîng-iú   sī   Ing-kok-lâng

<u>He</u> <u>often</u> <u>writes</u> <u>letters</u> <u>to</u> her.
tiānn-tiānn siá phue   hōo

VOCABULARY | Gí-sû 語詞

 Audio 3-2

WORD	MEANING	RELATED WORDS	MEANING
i 伊	he/she, him/her	i ê 伊 的	his, her, hers
		in individual	they, them; his/her
		in ê individual 的	their, theirs
ē-hiáu / ē-hiáng 會曉	to know how to do (*sth that must be learned*), can	bē-hiáu / buē-hiáng 袂曉	can't (not knowing how to)
		ē 會	can, will likely *(future tense marker)*; to become/get/feel + *adj*
		bē / buē 袂	can't, won't *(future tense marker)*; to not be/get/feel + *adj*
kóng 講	to speak (language); to tell (story, joke, lie)	kóng-uē 講話	to talk, to speak
		uē 話	spoken words, speech, language
		kóng tiān-uē 講 電話	to talk on the phone
Ing-gí / Ing-gú 英語	English (language)	Ing-bûn 英文	English (language; written language)
		Tâi-gí / Tâi-gú 台語	Taiwanese (language)
		Tâi-uân-uē 台灣話	Taiwanese (language)
		Jit-gí / Jit-pún-uē Lit-gí / Lit-pún-uē 日語 / 日本話	Japanese (language)

SHORT TAKES

WORD	MEANING	RELATED WORDS	MEANING
lú pîng-iú 女朋友	girlfriend	tsa-bóo pîng-iú 查某 朋友	girlfriend; female friend
		lâm pîng-iú 男 朋友	boyfriend
		tsa-poo pîng-iú 查埔 朋友	boyfriend; male friend
sī 是	to be; yes, right, correct	m̄ sī 毋是	to not be, isn't, aren't; no, wrong
		sī-m̄-sī…? 是毋是… ?	Is it / are you…? (yes or no)
		kám sī…? 敢 是… ?	Is it / are you… ? (question the idea)
Ing-kok-lâng 英國人	British (people)	lâng 人	person, people; human
		Tâi-uân-lâng 台灣人	Taiwanese (people)
		Huat-kok-lâng 法國人	French (people)
		guā-kok-lâng 外國人	foreigner
tiānn-tiānn 定定	often, frequently	hán-tit 罕得	seldom, rarely

He can speak English.

WORD	MEANING	RELATED WORDS	MEANING
siá phue 寫 批	to write a letter	siá 寫	to write
		phue 批	letter
		tsit tiunn phue 一 張 批	a letter ("tiunn": *measure word* for paper sheets or letters)
		tiān-tsú phue 電子 批	email
hōo 予	to give **hōo** + *sb* + *sth*	*verb* (send, bring) + *sth* + **hōo** + *sb*	to (someone)
		hōo + *sb*/*sth* + *verb*	to let, allow (*sb* to do *sth*); to be *verb*(**-ed**) by

REVIEW | Ho̍k-si̍p 復習

Listen to **Audio 3-3** and read the story in Taiwanese.

I ē-hiáu kóng Ing-gí.
伊 會 曉 講 英語。

I ê lú pîng-iú sī Ing-kok-lâng.
伊 的 女 朋友 是 英國人。

I tiānn-tiānn siá phue hōo--i.
伊 定定 寫 批 予 伊。

Translation

He can speak English.

His girlfriend is British.

He often writes letters to her.

DID YOU KNOW… | Lí kám tsai-iánn… 你敢知影…

All Taiwanese have to learn English at school. It's one of the five subjects in the Comprehensive Assessment Program for Junior High School Students, or the so-called **kok-tiong huē-khó** 國中會考, which is an exam most students have to take in their final year of **kok-tiong** 國中 (junior high school, grades 7-9) in order to enroll in **ko-tiong** 高中 (senior high school, grades 10-12). The other four subjects of the exam are: **Sòo-ha̍k** 數學 (Math), **Tsū-jiân** 自然 (Natural Sciences), **Siā-huē** 社會 (Social Studies), and **Kok-gí** 國語 (National Language).

Kok-gí 國語 is generally understood as Mandarin Chinese in Taiwan's current context but there has always been controversy surrounding this term. For centuries, Taiwan has been a multilingual society, with Taiwanese serving as the lingua franca. Back in 1946 when the Chinese Nationalist government arrived and started to promote Mandarin as "the national language", few in Taiwan could speak it. Since 2019, when the *National Languages Development Act* came into effect, Taiwanese and Hakka, along with indigenous languages, have all become officially recognized as "national languages", and so the idea of Mandarin Chinese as **Kok-gí** 國語 is being challenged more and more.

Japanese is the second most popular foreign language (after English) for Taiwanese to study. Apart from cultural and geographical reasons, there is also a historical one: Taiwan used to be part of Japan between 1895-1945, during which the term **Kok-gí** 國語 was also used by the government to refer to the Japanese language. This also helps to explain why there are many Japanese loanwords in Taiwanese.

EXERCISES | Liān-si̍p 練習

E01 Match each Taiwanese word to its English translation.

1. lú pîng-iú   ____   (a) to give
2. Ing-kok-lâng   ____   (b) to write a letter
3. kóng   ____   (c) British (people)
4. hōo   ____   (d) English (language)
5. siá phue   ____   (e) he/she, him/her
6. i   ____   (f) girlfriend
7. Ing-gí   ____   (g) to know how to, can
8. sī   ____   (h) often
9. ē-hiáu   ____   (i) to speak; to tell
10. tiānn-tiānn   ____   (j) to be; yes, right, correct

E02 Translate the sentences into English.

1. Guá ē-hiáu kóng Tâi-gí.

   _____.

2. I ê pîng-iú sī Huat-kok-lâng.

   _____.

3. Guá tiānn-tiānn siá phue hōo--in.

   _____.

4. I m̄ sī guá ê lâm pîng-iú.

   _____.

He can speak English.

LESSON 03

E03 Fill in the blanks with one of the words you've learned in this lesson.

1. Guá ê káu (   ) siû-tsuí.
   My dog knows how to swim.

2. I (   ) tsē hué-tshia.
   She takes trains frequently.

3. Guá (   ) tsin tsē phue.
   I wrote many letters.

4. Guá āu lé-pài ē siá phue (   )--lí.
   I will write a letter to you next week.

E04 Can you figure out how to say...?

Take a look at the vocabulary list and see if you can figure out how to say these sentences in Taiwanese:

1. "They can't speak Japanese."
2. "I seldom talk on the phone."
3. "Are they foreigners?"

Listen to **Audio 3-4** and see how you did!

LESSON 04

My grandma lives in Tainan City.

Picture the short scene described in English below, and then try to associate the underlined words with the Taiwanese translation.

 Audio 4-1

My <u>grandma</u> lives <u>in</u> <u>Tainan City</u>.
    a-má   tī Tâi-lâm-tshī

Her <u>house</u> has <u>3</u> <u>floors</u>.
    tshù   sann lâu

She <u>has</u> <u>6</u> <u>cats</u>. They are so <u>cute</u>!
    tshī la̍k niau-á   kóo-tsui

VOCABULARY | Gí-sû 語詞

Audio 4-2

WORD	MEANING	RELATED WORDS	MEANING
a-má 阿媽	grandma	a-kong 阿公	grandpa
tī 佇	at/in; to be at/in	(tī-)leh / teh (佇) 咧	to be verb(**-ing**) / to be present at (*location*)
		tī-leh / **teh** + *verb or location*	
Tâi-lâm-tshī 台南市	Tainan City	too-tshī 都市	(big) city
		Tâi-pak-tshī 台北市	Taipei City
		Tâi-tiong-tshī 台中市	Taichung City
		Ko-hiông-tshī 高雄市	Kaohsiung City
tshù 厝	house	tsit king tshù 一間厝	a house ("king": *measure word* for rooms, houses, schools, stores, etc.)
		tshù--lí / tshù--nih 厝裡	in the house; at home
		tshù-lāi 厝內	inside the house; at home; one's household
		tshù-pinn 厝邊	neighbor; neighborhood
		tshù-tíng 厝頂	roof
		khí-tshù 起厝	to build a house

WORD	MEANING	RELATED WORDS	MEANING
		puann-tshù 搬厝	to move (house); house moving
sann 三	three	sann-tǹg 三頓	three meals
lâu 樓	floor; multi-story building	tsi̍t tòng lâu 一棟樓	a multi-story building ("tòng": *measure word* for buildings)
		nn̄g (tsàn) lâu 兩 (層) 樓	two floors ("tsàn": *measure word* for floors, levels and steps of stairs)
		jī lâu / lī lâu 二樓	second floor
		lâu-tíng 樓頂	upstairs
		lâu-kha 樓跤	downstairs
		hō 號	number
tshī 飼	to feed, to raise (animal, child)	tshī kiánn / tshī gín-á 飼囝 / 飼囡仔	to raise children
la̍k 六	six	sòo-jī / sòo-lī 數字	number, figure, numeral
niau-á 貓仔	cat, kitty	niau 貓	cat
kóo-tsui 古錐	cute, adorable (child, pet)	khó-ài 可愛	lovable
		kuai 乖	tame, obedient, well-behaved (child, animal)

My grandma lives in Tainan City.

REVIEW | Ho̍k-si̍p 復習

Listen to **Audio 4-3** and read the story in Taiwanese.

Guán a-má tuà tī Tâi-lâm-tshī.
阮阿媽蹛佇台南市。

I ê tshù ū sann lâu.
伊的厝有三樓。

I tshī la̍k tsiah niau-á, tsiok kóo-tsui!
伊飼六隻貓仔，足古錐！

Translation
My grandma lives in Tainan City.
Her house has 3 floors.
She has 6 cats. They are so cute!

DID YOU KNOW... | Lí kám tsai-iánn... 你敢知影…

The six largest cities in Taiwan are often referred to as **La̍k-too** 六都. From north to south, they are: **Sin-pak-tshī** 新北市 (New Taipei City), **Tâi-pak** 台北 (Taipei), **Thô-hn̂g** 桃園 (Taoyuan), **Tâi-tiong** 台中 (Taichung), **Tâi-lâm** 台南 (Tainan), and **Ko-hiông** 高雄 (Kaohsiung).

The Greater Taipei Area, which includes **Tâi-pak** 台北, **Sin-pak-tshī** 新北市, and **Ke-lâng** 基隆 (Keelung), is the largest metropolitan area in Taiwan, with a population of 7 million (2019) in an area of 2,457 km² (949 sq mi). Its population is roughly equal to that of the Greater London Area.

EXERCISES | Liān-si̍p 練習

E01 Match each Taiwanese word to its English translation.

1. niau-á _____ (a) six
2. Tâi-lâm-tshī _____ (b) cute, adorable (child, pet)
3. sann _____ (c) cat, kitty
4. tshī _____ (d) to feed, to raise (animal, child)
5. la̍k _____ (e) grandma
6. lâu _____ (f) house
7. kóo-tsui _____ (g) floor; multi-story building
8. a-má _____ (h) three
9. tī _____ (i) at/in; to be at/in
10. tshù _____ (j) Tainan City

E02 Fill in the blanks with one of the words you've learned in this lesson.

1. In ê káu mā tsin ( ).
   Their dog is also very cute.

2. I kóng i tiānn-tiānn siá phue hōo ( ).
   He says he often writes letters to grandma.

3. In lú pîng-iú ê tshù ū ( ) tsàn lâu.
   His girlfriend's house has six floors.

4. Guá kin-á-ji̍t tsē kè-thîng-tshia khì ( ).
   I took a taxi to Tainan City today.

5. A-kong ( ) lâu-kha leh phàu tê.
   Grandpa is making tea downstairs.

My grandma lives in Tainan City.

E03 Translate the sentences into English.

1. Lín a-**kong** tshī sann tsiah káu-**á**.

   _____.

2. Tshù-**tíng** ū nn̄g tsiah niau-**á**.

   _____.

3. Guán tshù-**pinn** sī Ko-hiông-**lâng**.

   _____.

4. A-**má** hōo guán tsi̍t tsiah tsiok kóo-**tsui** ê niau-**á**.

   _____.

E04 Can you figure out how to say…?

Take a look at the vocabulary list and see if you can figure out how to say these sentences in Taiwanese:

1. "Grandpa's dog is really well-behaved."
2. "I am at home."
3. "She lives at no. 3, second floor."

Listen to **Audio 4-4** and see how you did!

LESSON 05

Let's go to the night market!

Picture the short scene described in English below, and then try to associate the underlined words with the Taiwanese translation.

🎧 Audio 5-1

<u>Let's</u>   <u>go</u>   to the <u>night market</u>!
lán   lâi-khì   iā-tshī

There are so many people and it's so <u>busy</u>!
                                                             lāu-ji̍at

I want to <u>eat</u>   two bowls of <u>braised pork rice</u>
                 tsia̍h   lóo-bah-pn̄g

<u>and also</u> <u>drink</u> a <u>cup of</u> <u>watermelon juice</u>.
koh   lim   pue   si-kue-tsiap

VOCABULARY | Gí-sû 語詞

Audio 5-2

WORD	MEANING	RELATED WORDS	MEANING
lán 咱	we (including listener), us, our; you and me	lán ê 咱的	our (including listener), ours
		guán / gún 阮	we (excluding listener), us, our; my
		guán ê / gún ê 阮的	our (excluding listener), ours
lâi-khì / lǎi 來去	to be/get going (usu. I or we); to leave	Lán lâi-khì + *verb* 咱 來去...	Let's (go) + *verb*(-ing)
		lâi 來	to come (to)
		Lâi tsi̍t uánn mī. 來 一 碗 麵。	Bring me/I'll have a bowl of noodles. ("Lâi" can be used to order at a food stand or restaurant)
iā-tshī / iā-tshī-á 夜市 / 夜市仔	night market	se̍h iā-tshī 踅 夜市	to go for a stroll in a night market
		tshī-tiûnn 市場	market
lāu-jia̍t / lāu-lia̍t 鬧熱	bustling, busy, crowded, lively	lāu-jia̍t kún-kún / lāu-lia̍t kún-kún 鬧熱 滾滾	to be super busy and crowded; to bustle with noise and excitement

Let's go to the night market!

LESSON 05

WORD	MEANING	RELATED WORDS	MEANING
tsia̍h 食	to eat; to drink; to take	hó tsia̍h 好食	tasty, delicious
		tsia̍h-pn̄g 食飯	to have a meal; to eat rice
		tsia̍h-pá 食飽	to be full (after having eaten)
		tsia̍h-hun 食薰	to smoke
		tsia̍h io̍h-á 食藥仔	to take medicine
ló͘-bah-pn̄g 滷肉飯	braised pork rice	bah 肉	pork, meat
		pn̄g 飯	rice (cooked)
		bí-hún 米粉	rice noodles, rice vermicelli
		thng 湯	soup
koh 閣	and also, moreover; yet still; again; (not...) anymore	iáu-koh / á-koh 猶閣	still
		koh-tsài 閣再	once more, once again, over again
		iū-koh 又閣	again (usu. recurring event or repeated behavior); and also

SHORT TAKES

WORD	MEANING	RELATED WORDS	MEANING
lim 啉	to drink	lim tsuí 啉 水	to drink water
		lim tê 啉 茶	to drink tea
		lim thng 啉 湯	to eat/drink soup
		lim-tsiú-tsuì 啉酒醉	to be drunk
pue 杯	cup (of), glass (of)	sann pue tsiú 三 杯 酒	three glasses of liquor / alcoholic drink
		pue-á 杯仔	cup, glass
		uánn 碗	bowl (of)
		kuàn 罐	can, jar, bottle (of)
si-kue-tsiap 西瓜汁	watermelon juice	kué-tsí-tsiap *(trad.)* / kó-tsiap *(new)* 果子汁 / 果汁	fruit juice
		liú-ting-tsiap 柳丁汁	orange juice
		ông-lâi-tsiap 王梨汁	pineapple juice
		phông-kó / lìn-gooh 蘋果 / (りんご)	apple
		puàt-á / pàt-á 菝仔	guava
		kin-tsio / king-tsio 弓蕉	banana
		suāinn-á 樣仔	mango

REVIEW | Ho̍k-si̍p 復習

Listen to Audio 5-3 and read the story in Taiwanese.

Lán lâi-khì se̍h iā-tshī! Iā-tshī lâng tsiânn tsē, tsiânn lāu-jia̍t!
咱來去踅夜市！夜市人誠濟、誠鬧熱！

Guá beh tsia̍h nn̄g uánn lóo-bah-pn̄g,
我欲食兩碗滷肉飯，

koh lim tsi̍t pue si-kue-tsiap.
閣啉一杯西瓜汁。

Translation

Let's go to the night market! There are so many people and it's so busy!
I want to eat two bowls of braised pork rice and also drink a cup of watermelon juice.

DID YOU KNOW… | Lí kám tsai-iánn… 你敢知影…

Night markets, which are called **iā-tshī-á** 夜市仔, are an integral part of Taiwanese culture and nightlife. They are also the places where you can find lots of delicious street food at more than affordable prices. Throughout the island there are an estimated 300 night markets. A few of the more famous ones are **Sū-lîm iā-tshī** 士林夜市 in Taipei, **Lô-tong iā-tshī** 羅東夜市 in Yilan, **Hông-kah iā-tshī** 逢甲夜市 in Taichung, **Hue-hn̂g iā-tshī** 花園夜市 in Tainan, and **Lio̍k-ha̍p iā-tshī** 六合夜市 in Kaohsiung.

If you are in Taiwan, pay a visit to the local night market. You will likely find **ô-á-tsian** 蚵仔煎 (oyster omelettes), **tshàu-tāu-hū** 臭豆腐 (stinky tofu), **kuah-pau** 割包 (pork belly buns), **tsin-tsu ling-tê** 真珠奶茶 / **hún-înn ling-tê** 粉圓奶茶 (bubble tea), and much more!

SHORT TAKES

EXERCISES | Liān-si̍p 練習

E01 Match each Taiwanese word to its English translation.

1. lán   ____   (a) to eat
2. iā-tshī   ____   (b) watermelon juice
3. si-kue-tsiap ____   (c) to drink
4. tsia̍h   ____   (d) and also, moreover; yet still; again
5. lāu-jia̍t   ____   (e) cup, glass
6. koh   ____   (f) night market
7. lâi-khì / lǎi ____   (g) braised pork rice
8. ló͘-bah-pn̄g ____   (h) bustling, busy, crowded, lively
9. lim   ____   (i) we, you and me
10. pue   ____   (j) to be/get going

E02 Fill in the blanks with one of the words you've learned in this lesson.

1. Guá āu--ji̍t siūnn-beh (_____) se̍h tshī-tiûnn.
   I'd like to go to the market the day after tomorrow.

2. Kuânn-thinn tshī-tiûnn mā tsiânn (_____).
   The market is also very busy in the winter.

3. I kin-á-ji̍t bô tsah piān-tong, (_____) phàu-mī.
   He didn't bring his lunchbox with him. He's eating instant ramen.

4. Guá hán-tit lâi (_____).
   I rarely come to the night market.

LESSON 05

5. A-má bē-hiáu (   ) tsiú.
   Grandma can't drink. / Grandma can't hold her liquor.

6. (   ) lâi sann uánn ló̩o-bah-pn̄g.
   Three more bowls of braised pork rice, please.

E03 Put the words in the right order to make a sentence.

1. iā-tshī / ū / tsin / Tâi-lâm / tsē
   (Tainan has many night markets.)

   _____.

2. tsiảh / bô / hun / lim / guá / tsiú / mā / bô
   (I don't smoke and I don't drink.)

   _____.

E04 Can you figure out how to say…?

Take a look at the vocabulary list and see if you can figure out how to say these sentences in Taiwanese:

1. "I had a bowl of soup."
2. "The rice noodles are so delicious!"
3. "I want two glasses of orange juice."

Listen to 🎧 **Audio 5-4** and see how you did!

LESSON 06

Sorry, I have not been feeling well lately.

Picture the short scene described in English below, and then try to associate the underlined words with the Taiwanese translation.

🎧 Audio 6-1

Are you <u>free</u>　<u>Monday</u>　?
ū-îng　　pài-it　　--bô

How about　watching a movie with me ?
hó--bô?　　khuànn tiān-iánn

<u>Sorry,</u>　I have <u>not been feeling well</u>　<u>lately</u>.
pháinn-sè　　bô sóng-khuài　　tsuè-kīn

I'm going to see a <u>doctor</u>　<u>that day</u>.
　　　　　　　　　　i-sing　　hit kang

VOCABULARY | Gí-sû 語詞

 Audio 6-2

WORD	MEANING	RELATED WORDS	MEANING
ū-îng 有閒	to be free, available; to have time	îng 閒	free, idle
		bô-îng 無閒	to be busy (with); to have no time
pài-it 拜一	Monday	pài-jī / pài-lī 拜二	Tuesday
		pài-sann 拜三	Wednesday
		pài-sì 拜四	Thursday
		pài-gōo 拜五	Friday
		pài-la̍k 拜六	Saturday
		lé-pài 禮拜	Sunday; week; church service
		lé-pài-ji̍t / lé-pài-li̍t 禮拜日	Sunday
		tsi̍t lé-pài 一 禮拜	one week

WORD	MEANING	RELATED WORDS	MEANING
bô 無	to not have, to not exist, without; not, no; otherwise..., if not so...	ū 有	to have, to exist;
		ū + *verb*	to have/did + *verb*
		--bô? ...無?	*(question marker)*
		(ū) + *noun/verb/adj* --bô?	
		ū-îng--bô? 有 閒 無?	(Are you) free? (Do you) have time?
		ū tsînn--bô? 有 錢 無?	(Do you) have money?
		ū-iánn--bô? 有 影 無?	Is it true?
khuànn tiān-iánn 看 電影	to watch a movie	khuànn 看	to see; to watch, to look at; to read
		khuànn--kìnn / khuàinn 看見	to see, to catch sight of
		khuànn tsheh / khuànn tsu 看 冊 / 看 書	to read a book
		tsit tshut tiān-iánn 一 齣 電影	a/one movie ("tshut": *measure word* for movies, dramas and plays)
		tiān-sī 電視	television

Sorry, I have not been feeling well lately.

WORD	MEANING	RELATED WORDS	MEANING
hó--bô? 好無?	How about…? (Is it) okay? Sounds good? (*new*)	hó--m̄? 好毋?	How about…? (Is it) okay? Sounds good? (*trad.*)
		hó 好	good, fine
		pháinn 歹	bad, evil, wicked
		hó-khuànn 好看	good-looking, pretty; interesting (a good read)
		hó lim 好啉	delicious, tasty, to taste good (drinks)
pháinn-sè 歹勢	excuse me, sorry; to feel embarrassed/shy	sit-lé 失禮	sorry, my apologies
(lâng) bô sóng-khuài (人)無爽快	feeling unwell, sick	sóng-khuài 爽快	pleasant, comfortable, refreshing
		sóng 爽	pleasant, feeling good, cheerful, joyful (*informal*)
		phuà-pēnn / phuà-pīnn 破病	to get sick, to fall ill
tsuè-kīn / tsuè-kūn 最近	lately, recently	kīn-lâi / kūn-lâi 近來	lately, recently
i-sing 醫生	doctor, physician, surgeon	huān-tsiá 患者	patient

SHORT TAKES

WORD	MEANING	RELATED WORDS	MEANING
		pēnn-lâng / pīnn-lâng 病人	patient
		pēnn-īnn / pīnn-īnn 病院	hospital
hit kang 彼 工	that day	hit 彼	that + *noun*
		hit + *measure word* + *noun*	
		hit ê / he 彼 个 / 彼	that (one), that thing
		tsit 這	this + *noun*
		tsit + *measure word* + *noun*	
		tsit ê / tse 這 个 / 這	this (one), this thing
		kang 工	day
		ū tsit kang 有 一 工	(there's) one day

Sorry, I have not been feeling well lately.

LESSON 06

REVIEW | Ho̍k-si̍p 復習

Listen to Audio 6-3 and read the story in Taiwanese.

Lí pài-it ū-îng--bô? Lán lái khuànn tiān-iánn, hó--bô?
你 拜一 有 閒 無？咱 來去 看 電影，好 無？

Pháinn-sè, guá tsuè-kīn lâng bô sóng-khuài,
歹勢，我 最近 人 無 爽快，

hit kang beh khì khuànn-i-sing.
彼 工 欲 去 看醫生。

Translation

Are you free Monday? How about watching a movie with me?

Sorry, I have not been feeling well lately.

I'm going to see a doctor that day.

DID YOU KNOW... | Lí kám tsai-iánn... 你敢知影...

The Taiwanese language has taken in words and concepts from Chinese (Mandarin), Japanese, and at times also Western languages. For example, Taiwanese borrowed the concept of "Sunday" from Western traditions and refers to it as **lé-pài-ji̍t** 禮拜日, which literally means "the day of the church service". The names for the other days of the week are just formed by counting the days that follow Sunday: **(lé-)pài-1** (禮)拜一 (Monday), **pài-2** 拜二 (Tuesday), **pài-3** 拜三 (Wednesday) ... **pài-6** 拜六 (Saturday, or "the sixth day after Sunday").

Another everday Taiwanese word actually borrowed from another language is **pēnn-inn** 病院 (hospital), which comes from Japanese. In fact, other common medical terms like **huān-tsiá** 患者 (patient), **tsù-siā** 注射 (injection), **sàng-sòo** 酸素 (oxygen), and **bái-khín** 黴菌 (germs), also come from Japanese due to the introduction of technology and modern science during the colonial period in the early-to-mid 20th century.

EXERCISES | Liān-si̍p 練習

E01 Match each Taiwanese word to its English translation.

1. pháinn-sè   ____   (a) How about...? Okay? Sounds good?
2. hit kang   ____   (b) excuse me, sorry
3. pài-it   ____   (c) to watch a movie
4. ū-îng   ____   (d) that day
5. khuànn tiān-iánn ____   (e) doctor, physician, surgeon
6. bô   ____   (f) Monday
7. hó--bô?   ____   (g) feeling unwell
8. bô sóng-khuài   ____   (h) lately, recently
9. i-sing   ____   (i) to be free, available; to have time
10. tsuè-kīn   ____   (j) to not have, without; not, no

E02 Write down the seven days of the week in Taiwanese.

Mon	Tue	Wed	Thu	Fri	Sat	Sun

E03 Fill in the blanks with one of the words you've learned in this lesson.

1. Guá (   ) tiānn-tiānn phuà-pēnn.
   Lately, I have often been getting sick.

2. I ê lú pîng-iú lâng (   ), tsit-má leh pēnn-īnn.
   His girlfriend is not feeling well. She's in the hospital now.

3. A-kong tī tshù-lāi (   ) tsheh.
   Grandpa is reading a book at home.

Sorry, I have not been feeling well lately.

4. Pháinn-sè, lín iáu-koh ū king-tsio--(   )?
   Excuse me, do you still have bananas?

5. Tsit ê ông-lâi-tsiap tsiânn (   ) lim.
   This pineapple juice tastes really good.

E04 Translate the sentences into English.

1. Lán pài-sì lâi-khì Tâi-pak, hó--bô?

   _____.

2. Guá tsuè-kīn tsin ū-îng, khuànn tsin tsē tshut tiān-iánn.

   _____.

3. Hit kang huān-tsiá tsiok tsē, i-sing tsiok bô-îng.

   _____.

E05 Can you figure out how to say...?

Take a look at the vocabulary list and see if you can figure out how to say these sentences in Taiwanese:

1. "I am free this week."
2. "This movie is good/interesting!"
3. "How have you been lately?"

Listen to **Audio 6-4** and see how you did!

LESSON 07

Who's that lady in the picture?

Picture the short scene described in English below, and then try to associate the underlined words with the Taiwanese translation.

Audio 7-1

That <u>lady</u>   <u>in</u> the <u>picture</u> is   <u>pretty</u>!
sió-tsiá   lāi-té   siòng-phìnn   suí

<u>(May I ask,)</u> Is she your <u>younger sister</u>   <u>or</u>
tshiánn-mn̄g   sió-muē   iah-sī

<u>older sister</u>?
a-tsí

She is not my younger sister, nor is she my

older sister...She's my <u>mother</u> !
     lāu-bú   --lah

68

VOCABULARY | Gí-sû 語詞

 Audio 7-2

WORD	MEANING	RELATED WORDS	MEANING
sió-tsiá 小姐	lady; Ms	sian-sinn / sin-senn 先生	gentleman, sir; Mr.; teacher, doctor
		thài-thài 太太	madam; Mrs.; wife
		siàu-liân-lâng 少年人	young man
		koo-niû 姑娘	girl, lady (*trad.*, unmarried); miss; nun/Sister
lāi-té / lāi-tué 內底	inside (*noun/adv/prep*)	lāi 內	in, within, inside
		noun + **lāi**	in, within, inside the + *noun*
		sim-lāi 心內	in one's heart/mind, inwardly
		guā-kháu 外口	outside (*noun/adv/prep*)
		guā 外	outside; over, slightly more than (*number*)
		noun/number + **guā**	outside the + *noun*; over, slightly more than + *number*
siòng-phìnn 相片	photo, picture	tsit tiunn siòng-phìnn 一張相片	a photo ("tiunn": *measure word* for paper, letters, photos)
		hip-siòng / hip-siōng 翕相	to take a picture

SHORT TAKES

WORD	MEANING	RELATED WORDS	MEANING
		(hip-)siòng-ki / (hip-)siòng-ki (翕) 相機	camera
		siōng 像	portrait, picture, photograph
suí 媠	pretty, beautiful	suí-tang-tang 媠噹噹	very beautiful, very pretty (usu. female after getting dressed up or made up)
		suí tsa-bóo 媠 查某	pretty woman
		suí koo-niû 媠 姑娘	pretty girl
		bái 䆀	ugly, bad, awful
tshiánn-mn̄g 請問	May I ask...; Could you please tell me... (a polite expression to start a question)	tshiánn 請	please; to host, to treat, to offer someone food and drink
		Tshiánn-tsē. 請坐。	Please take a seat.
sió-muē / sió-bē 小妹	little sister, younger sister (trad.)	me-me / me--me 妹妹 / 妹妹	little sister, younger sister (new)
		sió-tī 小弟	little brother, younger brother (trad.)
		ti-ti / ti--ti 弟弟 / 弟弟	little brother, younger brother (new)

WORD	MEANING	RELATED WORDS	MEANING
iah(-sī) / ah(-sī) 抑 (是)	or	iah-bô / ah-bô 抑無	otherwise; if not so...
a-tsí / a-tsé 阿姊	big sister, older sister (*trad.*)	tse-tse / tse--tse 姊姊 / 姊姊	little sister, younger sister (*new*)
		a-hiann 阿兄	big brother, older brother (*trad.*)
		ko-ko / ko--ko 哥哥 / 哥哥	big brother, older brother (*new*)
lāu-bú 老母	mother (*trad.*)	ma-ma / ma--ma 媽媽 / 媽媽	mother (*new*)
		lāu-pē 老爸	father (*trad.*)
		pa-pa / pa--pa 爸爸 / 爸爸	father (*new*)
--lah 啦	(*particle* often used to express slight disagreement, impatience or persuasion)		

REVIEW | Ho̍k-si̍p 復習

Listen to Audio 7-3 and read the story in Taiwanese.

Siòng-phìnn lāi-té hit ê sió-tsiá tsin suí!
相片 內底 彼个 小姐 真 嬌！

Tshiánn-mn̄g i sī lín sió-muē, ia̍h-sī lín a-tsí?
請問 伊 是 恁 小妹，抑是 恁 阿姊？

M̄ sī guán sió-muē, mā m̄ sī guán a-tsí...
毋 是 阮 小妹、嘛 毋 是 阮 阿姊...

Sī guán lāu-bú--lah!
是 阮 老母 啦！

Translation

That lady in the picture is pretty!

Is she your younger sister or older sister?

She is not my younger sister, nor is she my older sister...

She's my mother!

DID YOU KNOW... | Lí kám tsai-iánn... 你敢知影…

You have probably noticed that kinship terms in Taiwanese can be really complex. For example, when addressing or referring to brothers or sisters, the birth order matters. It gets even more complicated when talking about extended family. The Taiwanese language makes a distinction between cousins who are the children of your father's brothers (i.e. having the same family name) and all other cousins (i.e. having a different family name) such as the children of your father's married sisters or any of your mother's siblings. So, to address or refer to a specific "cousin", you must know the gender, the relative age, and whether the relationship is along the paternal-fraternal line.

"Cousin"	Cousins with the same family name (children of father's brothers)		Cousins with a different family name (children of mother's siblings and father's married sisters)	
	male	*female*	*male*	*female*
older	tsik-peh-tuā-**hiann** 叔伯大兄	tsik-peh-tuā-**tsí** 叔伯大姊	piáu-**hiann** 表兄	piáu-**tsí** 表姊
younger	tsik-peh-sió-**tī** 叔伯小弟	tsik-peh-sió-**muē** 叔伯小妹	piáu-sió-**tī** 表小弟	piáu-sió-**muē** 表小妹

In addition, kinship terms in Taiwanese often have a great deal of variety due to regional and generational differences brought about through language change and contact. This is somewhat like how in English there are many terms for "grandmother" such as "grandma", "granny", "grammy", "memaw", "mawmaw", "nana", "gammy", "gram", "mimi", etc. In this book, we try to introduce the most commonly used variations.

EXERCISES | Liān-si̍p 練習

E01 Match each Taiwanese word to its English translation.

1. sió-muē   ____
2. sió-tsiá   ____
3. lāi-té   ____
4. a-tsí   ____
5. lāu-bú   ____
6. ia̍h-sī   ____
7. --lah   ____
8. suí   ____
9. tshiánn-mn̄g   ____
10. siòng-phìnn   ____

(a) pretty, beautiful
(b) little sister, younger sister
(c) big sister, older sister
(d) May I ask; Could you please tell me…
(e) photo, picture
(f) or
(g) inside
(h) mother
(i) (*particle* marking impatience, persuasion)
(j) lady; Ms

E02 Fill in the blanks with one of the words you've learned in this lesson.

1. Guán pîng-iú ê (_____) tsiok kóo-tsui!
   My friend's little sister is so cute!

2. In (_____) sī i-sing.
   Her mother is a doctor.

3. Pháinn-sè, (_____) lí ū khuànn-kìnn guán sió-tī--bô?
   Excuse me, have you seen my little brother?

4. Kè-thîng-tshia-lāi tsē tsi̍t ê (_____) koo-niû.
   In the taxi sat a beautiful girl.

5. Guán (_____) tshī ê káu tsin kuai.
   My big sister's dog is really well-behaved.

6. Lín ko--ko hit kang hip ê (   ) tsin suí.
   The pictures that your big brother took that day are beautiful.

7. Tsit uánn bí-hún-thng sī lí ê (   ) guá ê?
   Is this bowl of rice noodle soup yours or mine?

8. Thài-thài, guā-kháu tsiok juah, (   ) tshiánn-tsē--lah.
   It's hot outside. Come on in and have a seat, ma'am.

E03 Can you figure out how to say...?

Take a look at the vocabulary list and see if you can figure out how to say these sentences in Taiwanese:

1. "That gentleman is not her father."
2. "Please have a seat, sir."
3. "There's a young man outside."

Listen to **Audio 7-4** and see how you did!

LESSON 08

Picture the short scene described in English below, and then try to associate the underlined words with the Taiwanese translation.

🎧 Audio 8-1

He went to a <u>department store</u>   <u>yesterday</u>
                    pah-huè kong-si   tsa-hng

to <u>buy</u> two <u>Christmas</u> <u>sweaters</u>.
   bé   Sìng-tàn   phòng-se-sann

He <u>gave (as a gift)</u> the small one to his <u>wife</u>,
    sàng   bóo

and kept the <u>large</u> one for <u>himself</u> to <u>wear</u>.
             tuā   ka-kī   tshīng

He bought two Christmas sweaters yesterday.

VOCABULARY | Gí-sû 語詞

Audio 8-2

WORD	MEANING	RELATED WORDS	MEANING
pah-huè kong-si / pah-hè kong-si 百貨 公司	department store	kong-si 公司	company
		kám-á-tiàm 簝仔店	grocery store; small retail store that sells a variety of household items
		tiàm 店	shop, store
tsa-hng / tsǎng 昨昏	yesterday	bîn-á-tsài / miâ-á-tsài 明仔載	tomorrow
bé / bué 買	to buy, to purchase	bē / buē 賣	to sell
		bé-bē / bué-buē 買賣	buying and selling; business, trade
		sing-lí 生理	business, trade
		sing-lí-lâng 生理人	businessperson
		tsò-sing-lí / tsuè-sing-lí 做生理	to do/run a business
Sìng-tàn(-tsiat) / Sìng-tàn(-tseh) 聖誕 (節)	Christmas	Kám-un-tsiat / Kám-un-tseh 感恩節	Thanksgiving
		Bān-sìng-tsiat / Bān-sìng-tseh 萬聖節	Halloween
		Tsîng-jîn-tsiat / Tsîng-jîn-tseh 情人節	Valentine's Day

SHORT TAKES

WORD	MEANING	RELATED WORDS	MEANING
phòng-se-sann 膨紗衫	sweater, knitted garment	niá 領	(*measure word* for clothes like shirts, pants, skirts, etc); neck, collar
		tsit niá sann 一領衫	a piece of clothing
		tsit niá khòo 一領褲	a pair of pants
		tsit niá kûn 一領裙	a skirt
		sann-(á-)khòo 衫(仔)褲	shirts and pants, clothes (in general)
		tsit su sann 一軀衫	a set of clothes, a complete outfit
		phòng-se 膨紗	yarn
		tshiah-phòng-se 刺膨紗	to knit (with yarn)
sàng 送	to give (as a gift); to send, to deliver; to see *sb* off	sàng-lé 送禮	to give a gift
bóo 某	wife	ang 翁	husband
		ang-(á-)bóo 翁(仔)某	husband and wife, married couple
		in (nn̄g ê) ang-á-bóo 俹(两个)翁仔某	(they) the couple

He bought two Christmas sweaters yesterday.

WORD	MEANING	RELATED WORDS	MEANING
tuā 大	big, large, huge; to grow up	tuā-lâng 大人	adult
		tuā-hàn 大漢	big and tall (body); the older one (birth order); to grow up
		tuā-siann 大聲	loud; to speak loudly or rudely
		sè / suè 細	small
		tuā-sè / tuā-suè 大細	large and small; old and young
		sè-hàn / suè-hàn 細漢	short and small (body); the younger (birth order); in childhood
		sè-siann / suè-siann 細聲	in a low/soft voice
ka-kī / ka-tī 家己	oneself, one's own	ka-kī-lâng / ka-tī-lâng 家己人	people on one's own side, one of us
		pa̍t-lâng 別人	another person, other people
tshīng 穿	to wear, to put on	thǹg 褪	to take off (clothes); to fall out (baby teeth), to shed (skin)

REVIEW | Ho̍k-si̍p 復習

Listen to Audio 8-3 and read the story in Taiwanese.

I tsa-hng khì pah-huè kong-si
伊昨昏去百貨公司

bé nn̄g niá Sìng-tàn phòng-se-sann.
買兩領聖誕膨紗衫。

Sè niá--ê sàng in bóo,
細領的送伊某，

tuā niá--ê ka-kī tshīng.
大領的家己穿。

Translation

He went to a department store yesterday to buy two Christmas sweaters.
He gave (as a gift) the small one to his wife,
and kept the large one for himself to wear.

DID YOU KNOW... | Lí kám tsai-iánn... 你敢知影…

Since only about 6% of the population is Christian, Sing-tàn 聖誕 (Christmas) is not an official holiday and not as big a holiday in Taiwan as it is in many Western countries. Because there is no strong association with the religious underpinnings of Christmas, you're likely to hear holiday music and see colorful decorations not only in shops but also in public schools and government facilities. Unlike in the West, where Christmas Eve is a chance to spend time with the family, in Taiwan, many (especially young) Taiwanese celebrate the holiday by going on romantic dates, writing holiday cards to friends, or just getting together with friends for a gift exchange party.

He bought two Christmas sweaters yesterday.

EXERCISES | Liān-sı̍p 練習

E01 Match each Taiwanese word to its English translation.

1. sàng _____ (a) sweater, knitted garment
2. Sìng-tàn _____ (b) yesterday
3. bóo _____ (c) to give (as a present); to deliver
4. tuā _____ (d) oneself, one's own
5. phòng-se-sann _____ (e) Christmas
6. ka-kī _____ (f) department store
7. tshīng _____ (g) to buy, to purchase
8. pah-huè kong-si _____ (h) wife
9. tsa-hng _____ (i) to wear, to put on
10. bé _____ (j) big, large, huge; to grow up

E02 Fill in the blanks with one of the words you've learned in this lesson.

1. Sit-lé--lah, guá (　　　　) tsiok bô-îng.
   My apologies, I was so busy yesterday.

2. Guán tshù-pinn (　　　　) guán tsin tsē suāinn-á.
   Our neighbor gave us many mangoes.

3. In (　　　　) tsuè-kīn phuà-pēnn, tsia̍h tsiok tsē io̍h-á.
   His wife has been sick lately. She's taking a lot of medicine.

4. Kuânn-thinn tsiânn tsē lâng (　　　　) phòng-se-sann.
   In the winter, many people wear sweaters.

5. Guá pài-gōo (　　　　) tsi̍t kuàn Huat-kok tsiú, lí beh lim--bô?
   I bought a bottle of French wine on Friday. Do you want to drink it?

6. A-tsí (　　　　) tsit ê lâng tī lâu-tíng leh khuànn tiān-sī.
   My big sister is watching TV upstairs all by herself.

7. Guá beh tsit pue (　　　　) pue ê phōng-kó-tsiap.
   I want a large glass of apple juice.

8. A-má tshiah tsit niá (　　　　) hōo--guá.
   Grandma knitted me a sweater.

E03 Put the words in the right order to make a sentence.

1. khì / la̍k / kám-á-tiàm / bé / kuàn / i / kué-tsí-tsiap.
   (He went to the grocery store to buy six bottles of juice.)

   _____.

2. sè niá / hit / khòo / tsin / niá.
   (That pair of pants is really small.)

   _____.

3. tī / ang / in / tsò-sing-lí / iā-tshī-á.
   (Her husband does business at the night market.)

   _____.

4. Bí-kok / guá / tuā-hàn / tī.
   (I grew up in the US.)

   _____.

5. tsiânn / lín / kóng-uē / tuā-siann
   (You guys are talking really loudly.)

   _____.

LESSON 08

E04 Can you figure out how to say...?

Take a look at the vocabulary list and see if you can figure out how to say these sentences in Taiwanese:

1. "I gave her an entire outfit on Valentine's day."
2. "Tomorrow is Thanksgiving."

Listen to **Audio 8-4** and see how you did!

LESSON 09

It was a nice day in the morning.

Picture the short scene described in English below, and then try to associate the underlined words with the Taiwanese translation.

Audio 9-1

It was a <u>nice day</u> in the morning,
　　　　hó-thinn

<u>but</u>　in the afternoon <u>the wind picked up</u>
suah　　　　　　　　　thàu-hong

and it <u>rained</u>.
　　　lȯh-hōo

I had <u>gone out</u> without an <u>umbrella</u>,
　　　tshut-mn̂g　　　　　　hōo-suànn

and <u>got drenched</u>　<u>from head to toe</u>!
　　ak kah tâm-lok-lok　kui sin-khu

VOCABULARY | Gí-sû 語詞

Audio 9-2

WORD	MEANING	RELATED WORDS	MEANING
hó-thinn 好天	sunny (day), fair weather	hó 好	good, fine
		pháinn 歹	bad, evil, wicked
		pháinn-thinn 歹天	rainy (day), bad weather
		thinn-khì 天氣	weather
suah 煞	(to end up...) unexpectedly; but, contrarily, instead, however (placed after the *subj.*)		
thàu-hong 透風	to start blowing strong wind, to pick up	hong 風	wind
		hong tsin thàu 風真透	the wind is really strong; it's windy
		khí-hong 起風	to get/become windy
lȯh-hōo 落雨	to rain	lȯh 落	to fall, to go down
		lȯh-tshia 落車	to get off the bus/train, to get out of a car/taxi
		hōo 雨	rain
		lȯh-hōo-thinn / hōo-lâi-thinn 落雨天 / 雨來天	rainy day

WORD	MEANING	RELATED WORDS	MEANING
tshut-mn̂g 出門	to go out, to leave home; to go on a journey	tshut--khì 出去	to go out, to get out
		tshut-kok 出國	to go abroad, to leave the country
		mn̂g 門	door
hōo-suànn 雨傘	umbrella	tsit ki hōo-suànn 一枝雨傘	an umbrella ("ki": *measure word* for long items that can be held in hand such as pencils, forks, umbrellas)
		hōo-mua 雨幔	raincoat
		hōo-sann / hōo-i 雨衫 / 雨衣	raincoat; rain jacket, rainwear
ak 沃	to water (plants); to drench	ak-tsuí 沃水	to water (plants), to irrigate
		ak-hue 沃花	to water flowers, to water the garden
kah 甲	to the point/extent that; until *verb* + **kah** + *result*	tsia̍h kah tsiok pá 食甲足飽	to get very full from eating (to eat to the extent of feeling very full)
tâm-lok-lok 澹漉漉	to be dripping wet	tâm 澹	wet
		ta 焦	dry

It was a nice day in the morning.

LESSON 09

WORD	MEANING	RELATED WORDS	MEANING
kui-sin-khu / kui-sing-khu 規身軀	the whole body; from head to toe	kui-ê 規个	the whole, entire
		kui-kang 規工	the whole day, all day
		sin-khu / sing-khu 身軀	body

REVIEW | Ha̍k-si̍p 復習

Listen to **Audio 9-3** and read the story in Taiwanese.

Tsái-khí sī hó-thinn, e-poo suah thàu-hong lo̍h-hōo.
早起 是 好天，下晡 煞 透風 落雨。

Guá tshut-mn̂g bô tsah hōo-suànn,
我 出門 無 紮 雨傘，

Kui-sin-khu ak kah tâm-lok-lok!
規身軀 沃 甲 澹漉漉！

Translation

It was a nice day in the morning, but in the afternoon the wind picked up and it rained.

I had gone out without an umbrella,

and got drenched from head to toe!

It was a nice day in the morning.

DID YOU KNOW... | Lí kám tsai-iánn... 你敢知影…

During the summertime in Taiwan, especially on the west coast, there are often afternoon thunderstorms due to strong convection in the tropics. Such thunderstorms are called **sai-pak-hōo** 西北雨 in Taiwanese. They are very intense, with heavy showers, lightning and sometimes strong winds before it starts to rain, but usually they come and go within a short period of time.

Another weather phenomenon that often occurs in Taiwan between July and September is **tsò hong-thai** 做 風颱. **Hong-thai** 風颱, also known as "typhoons" in English, are mature tropical cyclones formed in the northwestern Pacific Ocean. They often bring in gales and heavy rainfall, and can result in floods and landslides. The verb phrase **tsò hong-thai** 做 風颱 means a typhoon is forming or is hitting (it's "typhooning").

EXERCISES | Liān-si̍p 練習

E01 Match each Taiwanese word to its English translation.

1. suah _____
2. lóh-hōo _____
3. ak _____
4. kui-sin-khu _____
5. hó-thinn _____
6. kah _____
7. thàu-hong _____
8. tshut-mn̂g _____
9. hōo-suànn _____
10. tâm-lok-lok _____

(a) to rain
(b) to start blowing strong wind
(c) sunny (day), fair weather
(d) umbrella
(e) unexpectedly; instead, however
(f) the whole body; from head to toe
(g) to be dripping wet
(h) to go out, to leave home
(i) to water (plants); to drench
(j) to the point/extent that; until

E02 Fill in the blanks with one of the words you've learned in this lesson.

1. Bîn-á-tsài sī (_____) áh pháinn-thinn?
   Is it a sunny day or a rainy day tomorrow?

2. In nn̄g ang-á-bóo e-poo beh (_____) khuànn tiān-iánn.
   The couple is going out to see a movie this afternoon.

3. I tsa-hng kóng beh lâi, kin-á-ji̍t (_____) bô lâi.
   Yesterday he said he would come, but actually he didn't today.

4. Hōo-lâi-thinn, bē (_____) ê sing-lí tsiok hó.
   On a rainy day, the umbrella seller's business is really good. / On a rainy day, umbrella sales are really good.

5. Lín sió-muē tshīng (_____) suí-tang-tang.
   Your little sister is dressed up so beautifully.

It was a nice day in the morning.

6. Guā-kháu sī teh (   ), sī--m̄?
   Is it raining outside?

7. Guá (   ) bô sóng-khuài.
   I hurt all over.

E03 Translate the sentences into English.

1. I kui-kang bô tshut-mn̂g.

   _____.

2. Guá ū tsah nn̄g ki hōo-suànn, tsit ki sàng--lí.

   _____.

E04 Can you figure out how to say…?

Take a look at the vocabulary list and see if you can figure out how to say these sentences in Taiwanese:

1. "The wind was really strong in the afternoon."
2. "It was raining in the morning, so I went out in a raincoat."
3. "I was so full this morning!" (I got so full after breakfast!)

Listen to **Audio 9-4** and see how you did!

LESSON 10

Your place is so far away!

Picture the short scene described in English below, and then try to associate the underlined words with the Taiwanese translation.

Audio 10-1

<u>Your place</u> is <u>so</u> <u>far away</u>!
lín tau　　　ū-kàu　hn̄g

I <u>walked</u> for 2 <u>hours</u> <u>before</u> I finally
kiânn　　　　tiám-tsing　tsiah

<u>arrived</u>.
kàu-uī

I <u>don't want to</u> come <u>next time</u>!
　bô ài　　　　　āu-pái　　--ah

VOCABULARY | Gí-sû 語詞

Audio 10-2

WORD	MEANING	RELATED WORDS	MEANING
lín tau 恁兜	your place, your home	tau 兜	one's place, one's home (usu. used with a possessive pronoun)
		guán tau / gún tau 阮兜	my place, my home
ū-kàu 有夠	so, extremely, terribly; to be enough	bô-kàu 無夠	to be not enough, insufficient; not ... enough
		kàu-gia̍h 夠額	to be sufficient (number, amount, degree); satisfactory
hn̄g 遠	far	hn̄g-hn̄g 遠遠	rather far; from far away, from/at a distance
		kīn / kūn 近	close, near
kiânn 行	to walk; to move (chess, train, ship); to run (machinery, devices, vehicles)	kiânn-lōo 行路	to walk, to go on foot
		tsáu 走	to run; to leave, to go away; to move around
		tsáu-lōo 走路	to run away (from creditors, etc); to be on the run
		sàn-pōo 散步	to go for a walk, to take a stroll

SHORT TAKES

WORD	MEANING	RELATED WORDS	MEANING
tiám-tsing 點鐘	hour	puànn tiám-tsing 半點鐘	half an hour
		puànn tiám-tsing kú 半點鐘久	for half an hour
		time + **kú**	for a duration of + *time*
		tsit tiám-tsing 一點鐘	one hour
		tsit tiám 一點	one o'clock
		hun / hun-tsing 分 / 分鐘	minute
		bió / bió-tsing 秒 / 秒鐘	second
tsiah 才	and then; only then; before finally…; just, only *precondition, subj.* + **tsiah** + …	m̄-tsiah 毋才	that's why; only then, so that
kàu-uī 到位	to arrive	kàu 到	to reach (place, time, quantity), to arrive at; up to
		uī 位	place, space, position, seat; *measure word* for persons (*formal*)
		tó-uī / toh 佗位 / 佗	where
bô ài 無愛	to not want (to), to not feel like; to dislike	ài 愛	must, to need to; to like; to feel like; (*noun*) love, affection

WORD	MEANING	RELATED WORDS	MEANING
āu-pái 後擺	next time; in the future	tíng-pái 頂擺	last time
		íng-pái 往擺	earlier times, once, sometime in the past
--ah 矣	(*particle* indicating an action is completed or a change of situation)	bô--ah 無 矣	to not have anymore, gone
		hó--ah 好 矣	done, finished, to be good now

REVIEW | Ho̍k-si̍p 復習

Listen to Audio 10-3 and read the story in Taiwanese.

Lín tau ū-kàu hn̄g!
恁 兜 有夠 遠！

Guá kiânn nn̄g tiám-tsing tsiah kàu-uī,
我 行 兩 點鐘 才 到位。

Āu-pái bô ài lâi--ah!
後擺 無愛 來 矣！

Translation

Your place is so far away!

I walked for 2 hours before I finally arrived.

I don't want to come next time!

DID YOU KNOW... | Lí kám tsai-iánn...

Taiwan is a small and walkable island. Well, it definitely is if you like walking and have a passion for challenges. The distance of a **khuân-tó lí-hîng** 環島 旅行 (round-island trip) is about 900–1200 km (560–750 mi). It typically takes between 25 to 60 days to walk, according to many people who have done so.

A **khuân-tó lí-hîng** 環島 旅行, whether on foot, by bike, by motorcycle, or even by train, is quite a popular activity among younger people and backpackers. In fact, a round-island trip serves as the main plot device in the Taiwanese movies *Island Etude* (2006) (練習曲), ***Din Tao: Leader of the Parade*** (2012) (陣頭), and the documentary *Go Grandriders* (2012) (不老騎士), which tells the story of 17 "grand-riders", all in their 80s, who challenge themselves to a **khuân-tó lí-hîng** 環島 旅行 by scooter.

EXERCISES | Liān-si̍p 練習

E01 Match each Taiwanese word to its English translation.

1. tiám-tsing   ____   (a) next time; in the future
2. kiânn   ____   (b) so, extremely, terribly; to be enough
3. --ah   ____   (c) your place, your home
4. āu-pái   ____   (d) to arrive
5. lín tau   ____   (e) hour
6. hn̄g   ____   (f) and then; only then
7. bô ài   ____   (g) far
8. ū-kàu   ____   (h) to walk; to move; to run
9. tsiah   ____   (i) to not want (to); to dislike
10. kàu-uī   ____   (j) (*particle* indicating action completed)

E02 Fill in the blanks with one of the words you've learned in this lesson.

1. Guá (_____) kiânn-lōo, guá beh tsē kong-tshia.
   I don't feel like walking. I'm going to take a bus.

2. (_____) tuà toh?
   Where do you live? / Where is your place?

3. Guán lú pîng-iú ê kong-si tsiânn (_____).
   My girlfriend's company is really far.

4. Tse lóo-bah-pn̄g (_____) hó tsia̍h, guá koh beh tsi̍t uánn!
   This braised pork rice is so tasty. I want another bowl of it!

5. In sió-tī āu kò gue̍h (_____) beh tshut-kok.
   His little brother isn't going abroad until next month.

SHORT TAKES

6. Tsē hui-**ki** khì Ji̍t-**pún** ài sann (   ).
   It takes three hours to fly to Japan.

7. Lán (   ) tsiah koh **kóng**.
   Let's talk about it next time. / Let's keep it for next time.

8. A-**kong** tshī ê niau-á tī tshù-lāi (   ) lâi (   ) khì.
   Grandpa's cat is walking to and fro in the house.

E03 Choose the right verb to complete each sentence.

1. Hit tiunn **phue**, lí (ài / ē / ē-hiáu) ka-kī siá.
   That letter, you need to write yourself.

2. Lín āu--ji̍t kám (ài / ē / ē-hiáu) lâi guán tau?
   Will you come to my place the day after tomorrow?

3. Guán **ko**--ko (ài / ē / ē-hiáu) tshiah-phòng-**se**.
   My big brother knows how to knit.

4. Kin-á-ji̍t (bô ài / bē / bē-hiáu) lo̍h-**hōo**.
   It won't rain today.

5. I (bô ài / bē / bē-hiáu) tsia̍h io̍h-á.
   He doesn't want to take medicine.

6. Hit ê siàu liân-**lâng** (bô ài / bē / bē-hiáu) tsò-sing-**lí**.
   That young man doesn't know how to do business.

E04 Can you figure out how to say…?

Take a look at the vocabulary list and see if you can figure out how to say these sentences in Taiwanese:

1. "My place is very close."
2. "We have arrived."
3. "Half an hour is not enough. It needs an hour."

Listen to **Audio 10-4** and see how you did!

LESSON 11

There are birds singing in the tree.

Picture the short scene described in English below, and then try to associate the underlined words with the Taiwanese translation.

 Audio 11-1

There are some <u>birds</u>   <u>singing</u>   <u>in the tree</u>.
tsiáu-á   tshiùnn-kua   tshiū-á-tíng

They all <u>seem</u>   very <u>happy</u>.
kánn-ná   huann-hí

I'm going to <u>climb up</u>   and sing <u>along</u>
peh--khí-lì   tsò-hué

<u>with</u> them!
kah

VOCABULARY | Gí-sû 語詞

Audio 11-2

WORD	MEANING	RELATED WORDS	MEANING
tsiáu-á 鳥仔	bird	pue / pe 飛	to fly
		tshù-kak-tsiáu / tshik-tsiáu-á 厝角鳥 / 粟鳥仔	house sparrow
		hún-tsiáu 粉鳥	pigeon
tshiùnn-kua 唱歌	to sing a song; singing	tshiùnn 唱	to sing
		kua 歌	song
		tsit tiâu kua 一 條 歌	a song ("tiâu": *measure word* for streets, rivers, rope, thread, songs)
tshiū-á 樹仔	tree	tsit tsâng tshiū-á 一 欉 樹仔	a tree ("tsâng": *measure word* for trees, shrubs, plants)
		hio̍h-á 葉仔	leaf
		tshiū-nâ 樹林	woods, forest
		tik-(á-)nâ 竹(仔)林	bamboo grove, bamboo forest

There are birds singing in the tree.

LESSON 11

WORD	MEANING	RELATED WORDS	MEANING
tíng 頂	on, on the top of, above; (*measure word* for hats)	toh-tíng 桌頂	on the table; on the desk
		thinn-tíng 天頂	in the sky; in heaven
		tíng-kuân 頂懸	on, above, upside (*noun/adv/prep*)
		kha 跤	legs and feet, lower limb; under, underneath
		tshiū-á-kha 樹仔跤	under the tree
		ē-kha 下跤	under, underneath, underside (*noun/adv/prep*)
kánn-ná 敢若	to seem like, as if, likely		
huann-hí 歡喜	happy, delighted, glad	siong-sim 傷心	sad, grieved, heart-broken
		kan-khóo 艱苦	suffering, miserable
		huân-ló 煩惱	worried, to be anxious about
peh 跖	to climb, to ascend	peh-suann 跖山	to climb a mountain; mountain hiking
		peh lâu-thui 跖 樓梯	to go up the stairs

SHORT TAKES

WORD	MEANING	RELATED WORDS	MEANING
khí--lì / khí--khì 起去	to go up; to go up north; up *verb* + --khí-lì	peh--khí-lì / peh--khí-khì 距 起去	to climb up (away from the speaker)
		khí--lâi 起來 *verb* + --khí-lâi	to come up, to get up; up
		lóh--khì / lueh 落去 *verb* + --lóh-khì	to go down; to go down south; down
		lóh--lâi / luaih 落來 *verb* + --lóh-lâi	to come down; down
		pue--lóh-lâi / pe--lóh-lâi 飛 落來 *verb* + --lóh-lâi	to fly down (towards the speaker)
tsò-hué / tsuè-hé 做伙	together, jointly; to get along, to be together	tàu-tīn 鬥陣	together, jointly; to get along, to be together
kah 佮	with, and; to go together, to come with, to be added to, to attach	lí kah guá 你 佮 我	you and me
		Guá kah lí lâi-khì. 我 佮 你 來去。	I'll come with you.

There are birds singing in the tree.

REVIEW | Ho̍k-si̍p 復習

Listen to Audio 11-3 and read the story in Taiwanese.

Tshiū-á-tíng ū tsiáu-á teh tshiùnn-kua.
樹仔頂 有 鳥仔 咧 唱歌。

In kánn-ná tsiok huann-hí.
伊敢若 足 歡喜。

Guá beh peh-khí-lì kah in tsò-hué tshiùnn!
我 欲 𬦰起去 佮 伊 做伙 唱！

Translation

There are some birds singing in the tree.
They all seem very happy.
I'm going to climb up and sing along with them!

DID YOU KNOW... | Lí kám tsai-iánn... 你敢知影...

Taiwan is home to a wide variety of species—more than 600 species of birds and 4000 species of plants have been recorded in Taiwan. Some of the more colorful birds endemic to the island include: the Taiwan blue magpie (*Urocissa caerulea*) **tn̂g-bué suann-niû** 長尾山娘, or literally the "long-tailed mountain lady", the Mikado pheasant (*Syrmaticus mikado*) **oo-thī-ke** 烏雉雞, which is named in honor of the Emperor of Japan, and the Taoist priest bird (*Machlolophus holsti*) **sai-kong-á-tsiáu** 司公仔鳥, named perhaps because of its yellow and blue plumage which resembles a Taoist priest's robes. The two beautiful birds you can see on a NT$1000 bank note are Mikado pheasants.

SHORT TAKES

EXERCISES | Liān-sip 練習

E01 Match each Taiwanese word to its English translation.

1. tsò-hué _____ (a) to sing a song; singing
2. tsiáu-á _____ (b) tree
3. kah _____ (c) together, jointly
4. tshiùnn-kua _____ (d) to go up; up
5. peh _____ (e) to seem like, as if
6. tshiū-á _____ (f) with, and
7. tíng _____ (g) to climb, to ascend
8. khí--lì _____ (h) happy, delighted, glad
9. kánn-ná _____ (i) on, on the top of, above
10. huann-hí _____ (j) bird

E02 Fill in the blanks with one of the words you've learned in this lesson.

1. Guán lâm pîng-iú bô ài (   ) guá khì sèh pah-huè kong-si.
   My boyfriend doesn't want to go shopping with me at the department store.

2. Lán āu-pái (   ) khì in tau tsiah-pn̄g.
   Let's go to her place and have a meal together next time.

3. Toh-(   ) ū tsit tiunn siòng-phìnn.
   There's a photo on the table.

4. Guá sàng ti-ti tsit ê hip-siòng-ki, i ū-kàu (   )!
   I gave my little brother a camera. He was so happy!

5. A-má tshī lak tsiah niau-á, nn̄g tsiah (   ).
   Grandma has six cats, two birds.

There are birds singing in the tree.

LESSON 11

6. Guá tuà la̍k lâu, ài (   ) tsiok tsē lâu-thui.
   I live on the sixth floor. I need to climb so many stairs.

7. (   ) beh lo̍h-hōo--ah. Lí ū tsah hōo-suànn--bô?
   It seems like it's going to rain now. Did you bring an umbrella?

8. Guá bîn-á-tsài ē tsē hué-tshia (   ) Tâi-pak.
   Tomorrow I will take a train to go up to Taipei.

E03 Put the words in the right order to make a sentence.

1. tsē / tshiū-á / tsit / tsin / tíng-kuân / tsâng / ū / tshik-tsiáu-á
   (There are many sparrows in this tree.)

   _____.

2. tàu-tīn / lâi-khì / lé-pài / peh-suann / lán
   (Let's go hiking together on Sunday.)

   _____.

3. tiâu / bē-hiáu / guá / kua / tshiùnn / hit
   (I don't know how to sing that song.)

   _____.

E04 Can you figure out how to say…?

Take a look at the vocabulary list and see if you can figure out how to say these sentences in Taiwanese:

1. "I'm singing with her under the tree." (She and I are singing under the tree.)
2. "He seems really sad."

Listen to **Audio 11-4** and see how you did!

LESSON 12

Picture the short scene described in English below, and then try to associate the underlined words with the Taiwanese translation.

Audio 12-1

<u>The day before yesterday</u> my <u>daughter</u>
tsȯh--jit   tsa-bóo-kiánn

<u>celebrated her birthday</u>. She <u>received</u> many
tsò-senn-jit   siu--tiȯh

<u>gifts.</u> There was also a <u>diamond</u>   <u>ring</u>.
lé-bu̇t   suān-tsiȯh   tshiú-tsí

<u>Who knows</u>   <u>who</u>   gave it to her <u>!</u>
m̄ tsai   siánn-lâng   --ê

My daughter got many gifts on her birthday.

VOCABULARY | Gí-sû 語詞

 Audio 12-2

WORD	MEANING	RELATED WORDS	MEANING
tso̍h--jit / tso̍h--lit 昨日	the day before yesterday	āu--jit / āu--lit 後日	the day after tomorrow
		āu-jit / āu-lit 後日	some day in the future
		tsìn-tsîng 進前	before; previously
tsa-bóo-kiánn / tsa̋u-kiánn 查某囝	daughter	kiánn 囝	son; child (of a person); (*diminutive suffix* indicating small or a little)
		hāu-senn / hāu-sinn 後生	son
		gín-á 囝仔	child; little boy or girl
		tsa-bóo gín-á 查某 囝仔	girl
		tsa-poo gín-á 查埔 囝仔	boy
tsò-senn-jit / tsuè-sinn-lit 做生日	to celebrate one's birthday; to give a birthday party	tsò / tsuè 做	to do, to make, to serve/act as
		senn-jit / sinn-lit 生日	birthday
		senn / sinn 生	to give birth, to be born; to breed, to produce, to grow

SHORT TAKES

WORD	MEANING	RELATED WORDS	MEANING
siu--tio̍h 收著	to receive, to have received	siu 收	to gather, to collect; to put away
		--tio̍h 著 *verb* + --tio̍h	*(resultative complement indicating the action is performed successfully or has a result)*
		kià 寄	to send, to mail; to entrust; to deposit
lé-bu̍t 禮物	gift, present	lé 禮	gift, present; rite, etiquette, courtesy
suān-tsio̍h 璇石	diamond	kim 金	gold, golden; money
		gîn / gûn 銀	silver; money
		tsio̍h-thâu 石頭	stone, rock
tshiú-tsí 手指	ring	tsi̍t kha tshiú-tsí 一 跤 手指	a ring ("kha": *measure word* for rings, boxes, suitcases)
		tshiú-khuân 手環	bracelet
		phua̍h-liān 袚鍊	necklace
		hīnn-kau / hī-kau 耳鉤	earring
m̄ tsai 毋 知	to not know; I wonder	tsai(-iánn) 知 (影)	to know

My daughter got many gifts on her birthday.

LESSON 12

WORD	MEANING	RELATED WORDS	MEANING
siánn(-mih)-lâng / siáng 啥(物)人	who	siánn(-mih) 啥(物)	what; what + *noun*
		siánn-huè / siánn-hè 啥貨	what
		siánn(-mih)-khuán 啥(物)款	what kind of; how
--ê 的	the one/person/thing that is... (*particle* indicating *sb/sth* already mentioned with an emphasis on a certain attribute of it)	(sī) + ... + --ê (是)...的	It was ... that (*particle* used to emphasize a specific detail such as time, manner, person or place of an action or event.)
		Sī i sàng--ê. 是伊送的。	It was given by him; It was him who gave it to me.
		Guá (sī) tsa-hng kàu--ê. 我(是)昨昏到的。	I came yesterday; It was yesterday that I arrived.

SHORT TAKES

REVIEW | Ho̍k-si̍p 復習

Listen to **Audio 12-3** and read the story in Taiwanese.

Tso̍h--ji̍t guán tsa-bóo-kiánn tsò-senn-ji̍t.
昨日 阮 查某囝 做生日。

I siu-tio̍h tsin tsē lé-bu̍t.
伊 收著 真 濟 禮物。

Koh ū tsi̍t kha suān-tsio̍h tshiú-tsí,
閣 有 一 跤 璇石 手指，

M̄ tsai siánn-lâng sàng--ê!
毋 知 啥人 送 的！

Translation

The day before yesterday my daughter celebrated her birthday.

She received many gifts.

There was also a diamond ring.

Who knows who gave it to her!

My daughter got many gifts on her birthday.

DID YOU KNOW... | Lí kám tsai-iánn... 你敢知影…

Nowadays many young Taiwanese people celebrate birthdays like in western cultures: they give cards and gifts, sing birthday songs, make wishes, blow out candles, and cut cake. However, these things have only become part of Taiwanese birthday customs in the last few decades. Traditionally, celebrations only took place for **tōo-tsè** 度晬 (a baby's first birthday) or when a person reached their 50th or 60th birthday (and then only each decade afterwards, i.e., when they reached 70, 80, etc.).

On birthdays, Taiwanese people eat **mī-suànn** 麵線 (thin salted noodles) or **ti-kha mī-suànn** 豬跤 麵線 (thin salted noodles with pig trotters) and boiled eggs. To celebrate the birthday of an elderly person, people often bring presents to the birthday person, and in return the person's family would hand out **siū-thô** 壽桃 ("longevity peach", a peach-shaped steamed bun) and **âng-ku-kué** 紅龜粿 ("red tortoise cake", a round pastry made of glutinous rice with a sweet filling) to relatives and family friends.

For a baby's first birthday, the family prepares some **sing-lé** 牲醴 (animal sacrifices such as chicken, duck, fish, pork, etc.) and **âng-ku-kué** 紅龜粿 to worship the gods and ancestors. Today, these are often substituted with other food and pastries. In addition, twelve objects are placed in front of the baby. It is believed that the first object grabbed by the child will predict his or her future occupation.

EXERCISES | Liān-si̍p 練習

E01 Match each Taiwanese word to its English translation.

1. tsa-bóo-kiánn _____
2. siu--tio̍h _____
3. suān-tsio̍h _____
4. m̄ tsai _____
5. --ê _____
6. siánn(-mih)-lâng _____
7. tshiú-tsí _____
8. lé-bu̍t _____
9. tsò-senn-ji̍t _____
10. tso̍h--ji̍t _____

(a) to celebrate a birthday
(b) diamond
(c) ring
(d) to receive, to have received
(e) the day before yesterday
(f) who
(g) (*particle* the one/person/thing that is...)
(h) daughter
(i) gift, present
(j) to not know; I wonder

E02 Fill in the blanks with one of the words you've learned in this lesson.

1. Guā-kháu hit ê tsa-poo gín-á sī (_____)?
   Who is that boy outside?

2. Guá (_____) kah in ang-á-bóo tàu-tīn khì peh-suann.
   I went mountain climbing with the couple the day before yesterday.

3. Lí khuànn tsit kha kim-(_____) ū suí--bô?
   What do you think? Is this golden ring beautiful?

4. Lín tuā-hàn (_____) tsiânn ài tshiùnn-kua.
   Your older daughter really likes singing.

5. Tse lāi-té (_____) sī siánn-huè?
   I wonder what's inside this.

My daughter got many gifts on her birthday.

6. Hit king kong-si tsò (　　　　) ê bé-bē.
   That company trades in diamond.

7. Lí kià ê phue, guá bô (　　　　).
   I didn't receive the letter you sent me.

8. I sàng lí siánn-mih sìng-tàn (　　　　)?
   What Christmas gift did she give you?

E03 Can you figure out how to say...?

Take a look at the vocabulary list and see if you can figure out how to say these sentences in Taiwanese:

1. "My son is celebrating his birthday the day after tomorrow."
2. "That necklace is (made of) silver."
3. "I don't know what kind of person he is."

Listen to **Audio 12-4** and see how you did!

LESSON 13

I was playing a game on my phone.

Picture the short scene described in English below, and then try to associate the underlined words with the Taiwanese translation.

Audio 13-1

I was <u>calling</u> you <u>just a while ago</u>,
     kiò   thâu-tú-á

didn't you <u>hear</u>   it<u>?</u>
         thiann--tio̍h   kám

<u>Oh really?</u>   Sorry, I didn't <u>notice</u>. I was so
ū-iánn--ooh   tsù-ì

<u>drawn into</u> <u>playing a game on my phone</u>,
kòo   sńg tshiú-ki-á

and was just <u>about to</u> <u>beat the level</u>!
             teh-beh   phò-kuan

VOCABULARY | Gí-sû 語詞

 Audio 13-2

WORD	MEANING	RELATED WORDS	MEANING
kiò 叫	to call; to summon; to tell/ask *sb* to do *sth*; to order (food)	kiò-tsò / kiò-tsuè 叫做	to be called
		kiò kíng-tshat / kiò kìng-tshat 叫警察	to call the police
		kiò i lâi 叫伊來	to tell him/her to come
		kiò tsi̍t uánn mī 叫一碗麵	to order a bowl of noodle
thâu-tú-á 頭拄仔	just now, just a moment ago	tú-tsiah / tú-á 拄才 / 拄仔	just now, just a moment ago
		tú(-á)-hó 拄(仔)好	just (in time), just right; it just so happens that...
thiann--tio̍h 聽著	to hear	thiann 聽	to listen to
		--tio̍h 著	(*resultative complement* indicating the action is performed successfully or has a result)
		khuànn 看	to look
		khuànn--tio̍h 看著	to see
		thiann-kóng 聽講	to hear of; it's said that...

WORD	MEANING	RELATED WORDS	MEANING
kám 敢	(*question marker* to form rhetorical and general questions) *subj.* + **kám** + ...?	kám ū 敢 有	Did it...? Has it...? Does it have...?
		kám ē 敢 會	Will it...? Is it...?
		Kám án-ne? / Kám án-ni? 敢 按呢?	Is that so?
		kám-kóng 敢講	Is it possible that...; Can it be that...?
ū-iánn--ooh 有影 喔	Oh, really?	ū-iánn 有影	true, real, genuine; truly, really, genuinely
		bô-iánn 無影	untrue, false; not really
		iánn 影	shadow; to glimpse, to take a brief look
		--ooh 喔	(*particle* indicating surprise or persuasion, sometimes requesting further confirmation of the statement made)
tsù-ì 注意	to pay attention, to notice; carefully, closely	sè-jī / suè-lī 細膩	careful, cautious
kòo 顧	to take care of; to be engrossed in sth, to be obsessed with sth	kòo gín-á 顧 囡仔	to look after the children
		kòo sńg 顧 耍	to care only about playing (without thinking about anything else)
		tsiàu-kòo 照顧	care; to take care of, to look after

LESSON 13

WORD	MEANING	RELATED WORDS	MEANING
sńg tshiú-ki-á 耍手機仔	to use a phone non-verbally (texting, reading, playing games, etc.); to be preoccupied with one's phone	sńg 耍	to play, to toy with; to have fun, to mess around
		tshiú-ki-á 手機仔	cell phone, mobile phone
		tsit ki tshiú-ki-á 一支手機仔	a cell phone ("ki": *measure word* for phone, nose, mouth, teeth)
		tiān-uē 電話	telephone; phone call
		sńg tiān-náu 耍電腦	to play computer games
		tiān-tōng 電動	electric-powered; game console; video game
		tsit tâi tiān-náu 一台電腦	a computer ("tâi": *measure word* for cars, machines and electronic devices)
teh-beh / tih-beh 咧欲	to be about to	kiōng-beh 強欲	almost, nearly + *verb* (usu. against one's will)
phò-kuan 破關	to beat the level/game	phò-sán 破產	to go broke, to be bankrupt
		kuan 關	checkpoint, pass; barrier, difficulty

REVIEW | Hȯk-si̍p 復習

Listen to Audio 13-3 and read the story in Taiwanese.

Guá thâu-tú-á teh kiò--lí, lí kám bô thiann--tio̍h?
我 頭拄仔 咧 叫 你，你 敢 無 聽著？

Ū-iánn--ooh? Pháinn-sè--lah, guá bô tsù-ì.
有 影 喔？歹勢 啦，我 無 注意。

Guá tú-tsiah kòo teh sńg tshiú-ki-á,
我 拄才 顧 咧 耍 手機仔，

tú-hó teh-beh phò-kuan--ah!
拄好 咧欲 破關 矣！

Translation

I was calling you just a while ago, didn't you hear it?
Oh really? Sorry, I didn't notice.
I was so drawn into playing a game on my phone,
and was just about to beat the level!

I was playing a game on my phone.

DID YOU KNOW... | Lí kám tsai-iánn... 你敢知影…

Taiwan has a vibrant gaming industry and market. In the 1990s, many PC games from Taiwan became huge hits all over the Sinophone/Chinese-speaking world. Some games were even later adapted into novels, comics and TV shows. One famous example is **Sian-kiàm Kî-kiap Tuān** 仙劍奇俠傳 (*The Legend of Sword and Fairy*).

A more recent hit in the global gaming market is **Detention**, a survival horror video game developed by Red Candle Games and released in 2017 on multiple platforms. Set in the 1960s when Taiwan was under martial law, or the so-called **Pe̍h-sik khióng-pòo** 白色恐怖 "White Terror" period, the game incorporates elements from Taiwan's history, culture and folk beliefs. A writer named Ling Jing published a novel based on the game. In 2019, a live-action film adaptation of the game was released, earning 12 nominations and 5 wins at the 56th Golden Horse Awards, Taiwan's version of the Oscars. A new TV series also based on the story will be released in December 2020 on Taiwan's Public Television Service.

SHORT TAKES

EXERCISES | Liān-si̍p 練習

E01 Match each Taiwanese word to its English translation.

1. tsù-ì ____
2. thâu-tú-á ____
3. thiann--tio̍h ____
4. kiò ____
5. ū-iánn--ooh ____
6. phò-kuan ____
7. kòo ____
8. sńg tshiú-ki-á ____
9. teh-beh ____
10. kám ____

(a) to hear
(b) to pay attention, to notice
(c) *(question marker)*
(d) to fiddle with the phone
(e) to beat the level/game
(f) to call; to tell/ask *sb* to do *sth*; to order
(g) Oh, really?
(h) to be about to
(i) to take care of; to be obsessed with
(j) just now, just a moment ago

E02 Fill in the blanks with one of the words you've learned in this lesson.

1. Guá ( ) kàu-uī--ah!
   I am almost there!

2. Lí kám ū ( ) lán ê kua?
   Did you hear our song? / Do you hear the people sing?

3. ( ) ū tsit tsiah niau-á peh-khí-lì tsit tsâng tshiú-á-tíng.
   A cat climbed up this tree just a moment ago.

4. A-kong ( ) guá khì kam-á-tiàm bé la̍k kuàn tsiú.
   Grandpa asked me to go buy six bottles of liquor at the grocery store.

5. In kui-kang teh ( ), m̄ tsai sī teh sńg siánn?
   They've been fiddling with their phones all day. Who knows what game they are playing.

6. I kóng-uē tsiok sè-siann, lí ài ( ) thiann.
   He speaks very quietly, so you will have to listen closely.

LESSON 13

E03 Translate the sentences into English.

1. Tse Tâi-gí kiò-tsò siánn?

   _____.

2. Lí ū-iánn khuànn-tio̍h i--ooh?

   _____.

3. Thiann-kóng i phò-sán--ah.

   _____.

4. Guá siūnn-beh bé tsi̍t tâi tiān-náu hōo guán tsa-bóo-kiánn.

   _____.

E04 Can you figure out how to say…?

Take a look at the vocabulary list and see if you can figure out how to say these sentences in Taiwanese:

1. "She told me to look after the kids."
2. "I just heard him calling the police!"

Listen to **Audio 13-4** and see how you did!

LESSON 14

Ong plays basketball every morning.

Picture the short scene described in English below, and then try to associate the underlined words with the Taiwanese translation.

 Audio 14-1

<u>Ong</u>   wakes up at <u>seven</u>   <u>every day</u>,
Ông--ê   tshit   ta̍k-ji̍t

and goes <u>straight</u>   to <u>play basketball</u>
            suî   phah nâ-kiû

without <u>even</u>   eating <u>breakfast</u>.
       liân...to   tsá-tǹg

I don't know <u>how</u>   he has <u>so much</u>
             sī-án-tsuánn   tsiah-nī

<u>energy</u>.
khuì-la̍t

VOCABULARY | Gí-sû 語詞

Audio 14-2

WORD	MEANING	RELATED WORDS	MEANING
Ông--ê 王的	Ong (Ong is a common Taiwanese family name; "--ê": *suffix* for addressing or referring to a person, often indicating familiarity)	Tân--ê 陳的	Tan ("*family name* + --ê" usually refers to a man)
		family name + --ê	
		bē-tshài--ê / buē-tshài--ê 賣菜的	the person who sells vegetables; vegetable vendor
		verb + *object* + --ê	
		táng--ê 董的	chairman, director
		title + --ê	
tshit 七	seven	tshit-gueh-puànn / tshit-geh-puànn 七月半	The Ghost Festival (The 15th day of the 7th month on the traditional calendar; also known as "Tiong-guân 中元")
		tsit lé-pài tshit kang 一禮拜七工	seven days a week
ta̍k-jit / ta̍k-lit 逐日	everyday	jit / lit 日	day; the sun
		ta̍k-kang 逐工	everyday
		ta̍k-pái 逐擺	every time
		ta̍k-ke 逐家	everyone, everybody
		ta̍k ê 逐个	everyone; each one (of them)

SHORT TAKES

WORD	MEANING	RELATED WORDS	MEANING
suî 隨	to follow; right afterwards, straight away; each (...its own)	liâm-mi 連鞭	immediately, right away
phah nâ-kiû 拍 籃球	to play basketball	phah 拍	to hit, to beat; to attack, to fight; to cause (+ *result*); to play
		kiû 球	ball
		tsi̍t lia̍p kiû 一 粒 球	a ball ("lia̍p": *measure word* for roundish objects or granules such as balls, oranges, stones, pills and grains)
		iá-kiû 野球	baseball
		the-ní-suh / bāng-kiû （テニス）/ 網球	tennis
		phín-phóng / toh-kiû （ピンポン）/ 桌球	table tennis, ping-pong
		that kha-kiû 踢 跤球	to play soccer
		ūn-tōng 運動	to exercise; sports
liân...to / liâm...to 連...都	even	Liân i to tsai. 連 伊 都 知。	Even he knows.
		liân 連	to connect; in succession; even also
		to 都	*adv* used in a clause with the idea of indeed, yet, still, even, all

Ong plays basketball every morning.

LESSON 14

WORD	MEANING	RELATED WORDS	MEANING
tsá-tǹg / 早頓 / tsái-khí-tǹg 早起頓	breakfast	tǹg 頓	meal
		tsia̍h tsái-khí(-tǹg) 食 早起 (頓)	to eat breakfast
		tsia̍h tiong-tàu(-tǹg) 食 中晝 (頓)	to eat lunch
		tsia̍h àm(-tǹg) 食 暗 (頓)	to eat dinner
		tsia̍h puànn-tàu-á 食 半晝仔	to eat brunch (*new*)
sī-án-tsuánn 是按怎	why, how come (*trad.*)	án-tsuánn 按怎	how
		uī-siánn-mih 為啥物	for what reason, why (*new*)
tsiah(-nī) 遮(爾)	so, such (like this) **tsiah(-nī)** + *adj*	tsia 遮	here
		tsia--ê 遮的	these; these ones here
		hiah(-nī) 遐(爾)	so, such (like that)
		hiah(-nī) + *adj*	so/that + *adj*
		hia 遐	there
		hia--ê 遐的	those; those ones there
khuì-la̍t 氣力	strength, energy	ū-la̍t 有力	strong, powerful
		tshut-la̍t 出力	to exert oneself; with all one's might
		tsia̍h-la̍t 食力	tough, demanding; serious (sickness or injury)

SHORT TAKES

REVIEW | Ho̍k-si̍p 復習

Listen to **Audio 14-3** and read the story in Taiwanese.

Ông--ê ta̍k-ji̍t tshit tiám khí--lâi,
王的 逐日 七 點 起來,

liân tsá-tǹg to bô tsia̍h, suî khì phah nâ-kiû.
連 早頓 都 無 食,隨 去 拍 籃球。

M̄ tsai i sī-án-tsuánn tsiah-nī ū khuì-la̍t?
毋 知 伊 是按怎 遮爾 有 氣力?

Translation

Ong wakes up at seven every day,

and goes straight to play basketball without even eating breakfast.

I don't know how he has so much energy.

DID YOU KNOW... | Lí kám tsai-iánn... 你敢知影…

Taiwan may not be so well-known as a leading nation in sports, but there are a few areas in which Taiwanese athletes frequently contend for the top positions in the Olympics and other international competitions. These sports include **Tâi-kûn-tō** 跆拳道 (Taekwondo), **giâ-tsio̍h-lián** 夯石輪 / **kí-tāng** 舉重 (weightlifting), **siā-tsìnn** 射箭 (archery), **phín-phóng** (ピンポン) / **toh-kiû** 桌球 (table tennis), and **ú-môo-kiû** 羽毛球 (badminton).

lá-kiû 野球 (baseball) has long been considered the national sport of Taiwan, with a long history starting in the Japanese colonial era. The award-winning Taiwanese film *Kano* (2014) captures this history by depicting the true story of a multi-ethnic (Han Chinese, indigenous Formosan, and Japanese) vocational school baseball team that begun the season as an underdog but fought all the way to the National High School Baseball Championship of Japan in 1931.

EXERCISES | Liān-si̍p 練習

E01 Match each Taiwanese word to its English translation.

1. khuì-la̍t   _____   (a) breakfast
2. tsiah(-nī)   _____   (b) even
3. sī-án-tsuánn   _____   (c) seven
4. tsá-tǹg   _____   (d) why, how come
5. phah nâ-kiû   _____   (e) to follow; straight away
6. suî   _____   (f) strength, energy
7. liân...to   _____   (g) Ong
8. ta̍k-ji̍t   _____   (h) everyday
9. tshit   _____   (i) to play basketball
10. Ông--ê   _____   (j) so, such (like this)

E02 Fill in the blanks with one of the words you've learned in this lesson.

1. Táng--ê tsa-hng (_____) bô lâi?
   Why didn't our chairman come yesterday?

2. Ū--lah. I lâi bô nn̄g hun-tsing (_____) tsáu--ah.
   Yes, he did. He came for not more than two minutes and then left right away.

3. Guá kin-á-ji̍t bô-îng kah (_____) tiong-tàu (_____) bô tsia̍h.
   Today I was so busy that I didn't even have lunch.

4. Lán bîn-á-tsài (_____) beh tsia̍h siánn?
   What are we going to eat for breakfast tomorrow?

5. Lín kiánn uī-siánn-mih (_____) siong-sim?
   Why is your son so sad?

LESSON 14

6. In lâm pîng-iú beh khì Ing-kok (   ) kang.
   His boyfriend is going to England for seven days.

7. In e-poo kah Tân--ê khì (   ).
   They went to play basketball with Tan in the afternoon.

8. Guá tú-á khì ūn-tōng, tsit-má bô (   )--ah.
   I just went to exercise. I don't have any energy now.

E03 Choose the right word to complete each sentence.

1. Toh-tíng (tsit / tsia / tsia ê / tsiah-nī) ki tshiú-ki-á sī siánn-lâng--ê?
   Whose phone is this on the desk?

2. (Tsit / Tsia / Tsia ê / Tsiah-nī) sann sī beh sàng--lâng--ê.
   These clothes are to be given away as gifts.

3. Tshiū-á (hit / hia / hia--ê / hiah-nī) ū tsit liap tsiok tuā liap ê tsióh-thâu.
   There is a large piece of stone over there by the tree.

4. Khuànn i (hit / hia / hia ê / hiah-nī) huann-hí, guá mā tsin huann-hí.
   Seeing that she is so happy, I'm also very happy.

E04 Can you figure out how to say…?

Take a look at the vocabulary list and see if you can figure out how to say these sentences in Taiwanese:

1. "I will come right away."
2. "She is really strong."
3. "Ronaldo is a soccer player, not a tennis player!"

Listen to **Audio 14-4** and see how you did!

SHORT TAKES

LESSON 15

These red shoes are all pretty, but...

Picture the short scene described in English below, and then try to associate the underlined words with the Taiwanese translation.

Audio 15-1

I do <u>like</u>   this <u>pair</u> of <u>red</u>
kah-ì   siang   âng

<u>leather shoes</u>, <u>but</u>   they don't <u>fit</u>.
phuê-ê   m̄-koh   ha̍h

Those three pairs <u>off to the side</u> are also
pinn--á

really pretty, but they're <u>all</u>   <u>too</u>
lóng   siunn

<u>expensive</u>.
kuì

VOCABULARY | Gí-sû 語詞

Audio 15-2

WORD	MEANING	RELATED WORDS	MEANING
kah-ì 佮意	to find *sth* agreeable, to like	thó-ià 討厭	to find *sth* disagreeable, to dislike
siang 雙	a pair (of); two, even (number)	tsi̍t siang tī 一雙箸	a pair of chopsticks
		siang-tshiú 雙手	both hands, two hands
âng 紅	red; popular; to be at the height of one's career	âng-sik 紅色	red color
		âng-tê 紅茶	black tea
		âng-tsiú 紅酒	red wine
		âng-pau 紅包	red envelope (a monetary gift put in a red envelope given on the eve of Lunar New Year or special occasions such as weddings)
phuê-ê / phê-uê 皮鞋	leather shoes	phuê / phê 皮	skin, leather
		ê / uê 鞋	shoes
		bue̍h-á / be̍h-á 襪仔	socks
m̄-koh 毋過	but	...sī... m̄-koh ...是... 毋過	...does/is indeed..., but it's just that (usu. used to concede a point made but still with some reservation)

SHORT TAKES

WORD	MEANING	RELATED WORDS	MEANING
		Siok sī siok, m̄-koh bô suí. 俗是俗，毋過無媠。	It is cheap, but just not very pretty.
		iáu-m̄-koh / ah-m̄-koh 猶毋過	but, yet, however
ha̍h 合	to suit, to fit, to be in accordance with	ha̍h kha 合跤	to fit (one's feet)
		ha̍h-su 合軀	to fit (one's body)
pinn--á 邊仔	beside, next to; nearby; side	sin-pinn 身邊	at/by one's side; around oneself
		lōo-pinn 路邊	roadside
		lōo-pinn-tànn-á 路邊擔仔	street vendor, roadside stall
lóng 攏	all (of), both, together *quantifier/noun* + **lóng** + *predicate*	lóng-tsóng 攏總	(in) total, altogether; all
siunn 傷	too, overly	siunn tāng 傷重	too heavy
		tsia̍h siunn tsē / tsia̍h siunn tsuē 食傷濟	to eat too much
		sió-khuá-á 小可仔	a little, slightly; a small amount of

These red shoes are all pretty, but...

LESSON 15

WORD	MEANING	RELATED WORDS	MEANING
kuì 貴	expensive; valued; honored (+ *title*/*company*)	kuì-som-som / kuì-sam-sam 貴參參	to be very expensive
		sio̍k 俗	cheap
		tsînn 錢	money
		Guā-tsē tsînn / luā-tsuē tsînn? 偌濟 錢?	How much (money)?
		Kuí khoo gîn / Kuí khoo gûn? 幾 箍 銀?	How much? (lit. how many dollars?)

SHORT TAKES

REVIEW | Ho̍k-si̍p 復習

Listen to **Audio 15-3** and read the story in Taiwanese.

Tsit siang âng phuê-ê guá kah-ì sī kah-ì,
這 雙 紅 皮鞋 我 佮 意 是 佮 意，

m̄-koh bô ha̍h kha.
毋 過 無 合 跤。

Pinn--á hit sann siang mā tsiânn suí,
邊 仔 彼 三 雙 嘛 誠 媠，

m̄-koh lóng siunn kuì.
毋 過 攏 傷 貴。

Translation

I do like this pair of red leather shoes,
but they just don't fit.
Those three pairs off to the side are also really pretty,
but they're all too expensive.

DID YOU KNOW... | Lí kám tsai-iánn... 你敢知影…

When is the best time of year to shop in Taiwan? You may have wondered if there is a holiday like Black Friday, Boxing Day, or something like the Christmas shopping season. The closest equivalent would probably be **tsiu-nî-khing** 週年慶, which means "anniversary sale". It's typically held by department stores in October, but the actual period may differ from store to store. During this time, you may also see shoppers waiting in long lines early in the morning eager to snatch up deals when the doors open.

Another popular shopping time for many Taiwanese occurs the week before the Lunar New Year. It's when people go to buy special ingredients, traditional snacks, and gifts for relatives and friends. It's also the best time to observe the liveliness of traditional markets and shopping streets such as **Tik-huà Ke** 迪化街 (Dihua Street) in the **Tuā-tiū-tiânn** 大稻埕 (Dadaocheng) district in Taipei. The district was an important trading port and commercial area between the 19th and mid-20th centuries and has now become a major historical tourist attraction.

The Taiwanese-language TV series **Tsí-sik Tuā-tiū-tiânn** 紫色大稻埕 (*La Grande Chaumière Violette*, 2016) is set in the **Tuā-tiū-tiânn** of that period. It tells Taiwan's history through the lives of Taiwanese artists and their struggle as "Taiwanese" at the height of the Japanese colonial empire around the 1920s, towards the end of the Second World War, and at the start of Republic of China (ROC) rule.

The flashpoint of the 1947 二二八 事件 **Jī-jī-pat sū-kiānn** "February 28 incident" was also in **Tuā-tiū-tiânn**, in front of a tea house called **Thian-má Tê-pâng** 天馬茶房. A famous movie **Thian-má Tê-pâng** 天馬茶房 (*March of Happiness*, 1999) depicts a teenage love story against this tragic historical backdrop.

This district is also the setting for other popular Taiwanese dramas, such as **Siang-siânn Kòo-sū** 雙城故事 (*A Taiwanese Tale of Two Cities*, 2018), **Lāu-koo-pô ê Kóo-tóng Lāu-tshài-tuann** 老姑婆的古董老菜單 (*Recipe of Life*, 2020), and the eponymous film **Tuā-tiū-tiânn** 大稻埕 (*Twa-Tiu-Tiann*, 2014).

EXERCISES | Liān-si̍p 練習

E01 Match each Taiwanese word to its English translation.

1. âng _____ (a) too, overly
2. siunn _____ (b) all (of), both, together
3. kah-ì _____ (c) red; popular
4. kuì _____ (d) leather shoes
5. siang _____ (e) but
6. phuê-ê _____ (f) to suit, to fit, to be in accordance with
7. ha̍h _____ (g) a pair (of); two, even (number)
8. pinn--á _____ (h) expensive
9. m̄-koh _____ (i) to find sth agreeable, to like
10. lóng _____ (j) beside, next to; nearby; side

E02 Fill in the blanks with one of the words you've learned in this lesson.

1. Lí kóng-uē ( ) sè-siann, guá bô thiann--tio̍h.
   You were speaking too quietly, so I didn't hear it.

2. Hit niá kûn lí ū ( )--bô?
   Did you like that skirt?

3. Guán a-tsí tī pah-huè kong-si bé tshit ( ) bue̍h-á.
   My big sister bought seven pairs of socks at the department store.

4. Lîm--ê tsiok ài ūn-tōng, ta̍k-kang ( ) khì phah nâ-kiû.
   Lim loves sports. He goes to play basketball every day.

5. Guá tiong-tàu ū tsia̍h sī ū tsia̍h, ( ) tsia̍h bô tsē.
   I did have lunch, but I didn't eat much.

6. Tsit ki tshiú-ki-á sī-án-tsuánn tsiah-nī (   )?
   Why is this cell phone so expensive?

7. Guán tau tuà tī iā-tshī (   ).
   I live beside the night market. / My place is next to a night market.

E03 Translate the sentences into English.

1. Tsit niá sann bô hảh-su.

   _____.

2. Tsia--ê lóng-tsóng kuí khoo gîn?

   _____.

3. I ê phuê-ê sī lōo-pinn-tànn-á bé--ê.

   _____.

E04 Can you figure out how to say…?

Take a look at the vocabulary list and see if you can figure out how to say these sentences in Taiwanese:

1. "How much is that pair of shoes?"
2. "Red wine, black tea, (they) are both red."

Listen to **Audio 15-4** and see how you did!

LESSON 16

How long does it take for you to bike to the station?

Picture the short scene described in English below, and then try to associate the underlined words with the Taiwanese translation.

Audio 16-1

To <u>ride</u>   a <u>bike</u>   <u>from</u> here to the
khiâ   thih-bé   tuì

<u>train station</u>,   it <u>should take</u>   an <u>ordinary</u>
hué-tshia-thâu   tio̍h-ài   phóo-thong

person <u>45</u>   minutes.
si̍-tsa̍p-gōo

<u>As for</u> me, if I'm not there in under half an
iah nā

hour, <u>(then)</u>   you'<u>d better</u> call the police!
tō   hó thang

VOCABULARY | Gí-sû 語詞

 Audio 16-2

WORD	MEANING	RELATED WORDS	MEANING
khiâ 騎	to ride	khiâ-bé 騎馬	to ride a horse; horse riding
		khiâ-tshia 騎車	to ride a bike/vehicle
thih-bé 鐵馬	bicycle	kha-ta̍h-tshia 跤踏車	bicycle
		oo-tóo-bái / ki-tshia (オートバイ) / 機車	motorcycle, scooter
tuì / uì 對	from; to, towards, facing; as to, with regard to	Lí tuì tó-(uī) lâi? 你對佗(位)來？	Where do/did you come from?
		tuì + *location* + *verb (movement)*	*verb* + from + *location*
		I tsáu tuì tshī-tiûnn khì. 伊走對市場去。	He runs to/towards the market.
		verb (movement) + tuì + *location*	*verb* + to/towards + *location*
hué-tshia-thâu / **hé-tshia-thâu** 火車頭	train station	tshia-tsām / tshia-thâu 車站 / 車頭	station
		(kong-)tshia-pâi-á (公)車牌仔	bus stop (lit: the board for bus routes and timetables)
tio̍h-ài 著愛	should, need to, ought to	tio̍h 著	Yes, right; to be correct, to hit the mark; to achieve; to catch (a disease); should, need to, ought to
		m̄-tio̍h 毋著	wrong; to be incorrect
		bô m̄-tio̍h 無毋著	that's right; You are absolutely right!

SHORT TAKES

WORD	MEANING	RELATED WORDS	MEANING
phóo-thong 普通	ordinary, normal; usually, normally	kî-kuài 奇怪	strange, weird, unusual
		tik-piat 特別	special; specially, extraordinarily
sì-tsa̍p-gōo 四十五	forty-five	sì 四	four
		sì-kè / sì-kuè 四界	everywhere, anywhere
		tsa̍p 十	ten
		gōo 五	five
		gōo-gue̍h-tseh / gōo-ji̍t-tseh 五月節 / 五日節	The Dragon Boat Festival (The 5th day of the 5th month on the traditional calendar)
iah nā 抑若	as for; yet if it were	(iah) nā bô (抑) 若無	otherwise; if not so
		iah / ah 抑	or; as for, by the way (usu. used to introduce a different topic)
		nā 若	if
tō / tiō 就	then; just	Lí (nā) thiàu, guá tō thiàu. 你(若)跳，我就跳。	(If) you jump, I jump.
		(nā) *precondition* + tō + *predicate*	if... then; as long as

How long does it take for you to bike to the station?

LESSON 16

WORD	MEANING	RELATED WORDS	MEANING
		Guá gōo tiám tō khí--lâi. 我 五 點 就 起來。	I wake up as early as five o'clock.
		precondition + **tō** + *predicate*	as soon as; as early as, already
		tō sī / tiō sī 就 是	just, exactly; to be exactly sb/sth
hó (thang) 好 (通)	it's about time to; had better	thang 通	may, can; (in order) to, so as to
		m̄-thang 毋通	don't, had better not to
		bô pn̄g thang tsia̍h 無 飯 通 食	to have no rice/food to eat
		bô + *sth* + **thang** + *verb*	to have no + *sth* + to + *verb*
		ū tsînn thang bé / ū tsînn thang bué 有 錢 通 買	to have the money to buy
		ū + *sth* + **thang** + *verb*	to have + *sth* + to + *verb*

SHORT TAKES

REVIEW | Ho̍k-si̍p 復習

Listen to **Audio 16-3** and read the story in Taiwanese.

Tuì tsia khiâ thih-bé kàu hué-tshia-thâu,
對 遮 騎 鐵馬 到 火車頭,

phóo-thong lâng tio̍h-ài sì-tsa̍p-gōo hun.
普通 人 著愛 四十五 分。

Iah nā guá, puànn tiám-tsing bô kàu-uī,
抑 若 我,半 點鐘 無 到位,

lí tō hó thang kiò kíng-tshat--ah!
你 就 好 通 叫 警察 矣!

Translation

To ride a bike from here to the train station,
it should take an ordinary person 45 minutes.
As for me, if I'm not there in under half an hour,
(then) you'd better call the police!

DID YOU KNOW… | Lí kám tsai-iánn… 你敢知影…

Taiwan holds an important spot in the global cycling industry. If you're a bike lover, you've probably heard of some Taiwanese brands like Giant (捷安特), Merida (美利達) and KMC (桂盟). Considered the world's largest bicycle manufacturer, Giant makes high-end mountain bikes that are preferred by professional cyclists and also produces a large variety of road, hybrid and e-bikes. Merida is another global brand best known for its mountain bikes, while KMC is a roller chain manufacturer that makes a popular brand of bike chains.

Bicycles were introduced to Taiwan at the turn of the 20th century during the Japanese era. By the 1930s, one in three Taiwanese households owned a bike. Despite its long-time popularity, the "bicycle" goes by many different terms in Taiwanese. In addition to **thih-bé** 鐵馬 and **kha-tàh-tshia** 跤踏車, there are also **tsū-tsuán-tshia** 自轉車 or **tsū-lián-tshia** 自輪車, which originally came from the Japanese word 自転車 (*ji-ten-sha*, "self-rolling-vehicle"), and **khóng-bîng-tshia** 孔明車, which is more often heard in Taipei. This again reflects the diversity of Taiwanese dialects on the island.

EXERCISES | Liān-si̍p 練習

E01 Match each Taiwanese word to its English translation.

1. phóo-thong   ____   (a) to ride
2. hó (thang)   ____   (b) ordinary, normal; usually, normally
3. thih-bé   ____   (c) forty-five
4. tuì   ____   (d) then; just
5. tio̍h-ài   ____   (e) train station
6. hué-tshia-thâu ____   (f) it's about time to; had better... now
7. sì-tsa̍p-gōo   ____   (g) from; to, towards, facing
8. iah nā   ____   (h) should, need to, ought to
9. khiâ   ____   (i) as for; yet if it were
10. tō   ____   (j) bicycle

E02 Fill in the blanks with one of the words you've learned in this lesson.

1. Lí kám ē-hiáu (   ) oo-tóo-bái?
   Do you know how to ride a scooter?

2. Lí khiâ-tshia (   ) sè-jī.
   Be careful when you ride.

3. Guán **ang** tsin kah-ì hit tâi âng (   ).
   My husband really likes that red bike.

4. Guá (   ) tshit tiám **puànn** tsia̍h tsá-tǹg,
   tshit tiám (   ) hun tshut-mn̂g.
   I usually have my breakfast at half past seven, and go out at a quarter to eight.

LESSON 16

5. (　　　　　) guán tau kiânn khì kong-tshia-pâi-á bô tsiok hn̄g,
   gōo hun-tsing (　　　　　) kàu--ah.
   It is not very far to walk from my place to the bus stop; you will get there in just five minutes.

6. Kin-á-jit (　　　　　) tik-piàt lāu-jia̍t.
   The train station is extraordinarily busy today.

E03 Put the words in the right order to make a sentence.

1. m̄-thang / nā / siunn / tō / bé / kuì
   (Don't buy it if it's too expensive.)

   _____.

2. m̄-tio̍h / tíng-pái / uī / tsáu / guá
   (I went to the wrong place last time.)

   _____.

E04 Can you figure out how to say...?

Take a look at the vocabulary list and see if you can figure out how to say these sentences in Taiwanese:

1. "I will arrive at 4:15."
2. "I come from Korea."

Listen to **Audio 16-4** and see how you did!

SHORT TAKES

LESSON 17

I was hungry in the middle of the night.

Picture the short scene described in English below, and then try to associate the underlined words with the Taiwanese translation.

 **Audio 17-1**

I was <u>hungry</u>   <u>in the middle of the night</u>.
pak-tóo-iau   puànn-mê-á

But, when I <u>opened</u>   <u>the fridge</u>, wanting
khui   ping-siunn

to <u>find</u>   <u>something</u> to eat, I <u>only</u> found
tshuē   mi̍h-kiānn   kan-na

half a bottle of <u>milk</u>   that had <u>already</u>
gû-ling   í-king

<u>gone sour</u>.
tshàu-sng

148

VOCABULARY | Gí-sû 語詞

Audio 17-2

WORD	MEANING	RELATED WORDS	MEANING
pak-tóo-iau 腹肚枵	to be hungry	pak-tóo 腹肚	belly, stomach
		iau 枵	hungry
		pá 飽	full
		tshuì 喙	mouth; mouthful; opening
		tshuì-ta 喙焦	to be thirsty
puànn-mê(-á) / puànn-mî(-á) 半暝(仔)	in the middle of the night, midnight	puànn 半	half, semi-, mid-; in the middle of
		tsit-puànn 一半	a half, one half
		kui-mê / kui-mî 規暝	whole night
		tsa-mê / tsa-mî 昨暝	last night
		mê--sî / mî--sî 暝時	nighttime, during the night
		jit--sî / lit--sî 日時	daytime, during the day

SHORT TAKES

WORD	MEANING	RELATED WORDS	MEANING
khui 開	to open; to turn on; to start off, to set out; to issue (bills, checks, traffic tickets), to prescribe (medicine)	khui-mn̂g 開門	to open the door
		khui tiān-sī 開電視	to turn on the TV
		kuainn / kuinn 關	to close, to shut; to turn off
		kuainn thang-á / kuinn thang-á 關窗仔	to close the window
		kuainn tiàm / kuinn tiàm 關店	to close the store; to close up shop, to go out of business
ping-siunn 冰箱	fridge, freezer	ping 冰	ice; ice-cold
		siunn-á 箱仔	large box, chest, case
mih(-kiānn) / mn̍gh(-kiānn) 物 (件)	(material) things; object, item	bé mih(-kiānn) / bué mn̍gh(-kiānn) 買物 (件)	to buy things, to shop; shopping
		tsiah mih(-kiānn) / tsiah mn̍gh(-kiānn) 食物 (件)	to eat something, to eat; eating
kan-na 干焦	only, merely, no more than	m̄-nā 毋但	not only
tshuē / tshē 揣	to search, to look for	tshuē--tio̍h / tshē--tio̍h 揣著	to find
		tshuē-bô / tshē-bô 揣無	didn't find, couldn't find
		Tshuē-ū--bô? / Tshē-ū--bô? 揣有無?	Have you found it?

I was hungry in the middle of the night.

LESSON 17

WORD	MEANING	RELATED WORDS	MEANING
gû-ling / gû-ni 牛奶	milk (from cows)	gû 牛	cow, cattle
		tāu-ling / tāu-ni 豆奶	soy milk
		bí-ling / bí-ni 米奶	rice milk (a breakfast drink usually made with rice, peanuts and sesame)
í-king 已經	already	iá-buē / iá-bē 猶未	not yet
tshàu-sng 臭酸	to spoil (food), to go/turn sour	tshàu 臭	stinky, smelly
		sng 酸	sour, acidic; aching
		phang 芳	fragrant, aromatic, sweet-smelling, delicious-smelling

SHORT TAKES

REVIEW | Ho̍k-si̍p 復習

Listen to Audio **17-3** and read the story in Taiwanese.

Guá puànn-mê-á pak-tóo-iau,
我 半暝仔 腹肚枵,

khui ping-siunn beh tshuē mi̍h-kiānn tsia̍h,
開 冰箱 欲 揣 物件 食,

kan-na tshuē-tio̍h puànn kuàn í-king tshàu-sng ê gû-ling.
干焦 揣著 半 罐 已經 臭酸 的 牛奶。

Translation

I was hungry in the middle of the night.

But, when I opened the fridge, wanting to find something to eat,

I only found half a bottle of milk that had already gone sour.

I was hungry in the middle of the night.

DID YOU KNOW... | Lí kám tsai-iánn... 你敢知影…

Eating **siau-iā** 宵夜 (midnight snack) is a widespread practice within Taiwan's food culture. Many Taiwanese will have a fourth meal or small snack just before going to bed. If you're hungry in the middle of the night, don't worry! Simply visit any of the **iā-tshī** 夜市 (night markets) or **tiám-sim-tànn** 點心攤 (snack vendors), and you'll be sure to find something that will fulfill those late-night cravings. It shouldn't be too difficult to find a place that is open late into the night selling **kiâm-soo-ke** 鹹酥雞 (fried chicken), **hang-bah** 烘肉 (grilled meat skewers), **lóo-bī** 滷味 (braised meat or vegetables), or other Taiwanese street foods.

Another common sight you might come across as part of Taiwan's midnight snack scene is **Tāu-ni-tiàm** / **Tāu-ling-tiàm** 豆奶店, literally "soy milk stores". Most of them open early to serve breakfast, but some will start even earlier the night before to feed the late-night crowd. Apart from soy milk and rice milk, these places will typically offer a wide array of carb-heavy comfort food like **sio-piánn** 燒餅 (sesame flatbread), **iû-tsia̍h-kué** 油炸粿 (fried dough sticks), **nn̄g-piánn** 卵餅 (egg pancakes), **pn̄g-uân** 飯丸 (rice balls), **bah-pau** 肉包 (meat buns), **lâng-sn̂g-pau-á** 籠床包仔 (soup dumplings), and much more.

EXERCISES | Liān-si̍p 練習

E01 Match each Taiwanese word to its English translation.

1. tshuē _____
2. tshàu-sng _____
3. gû-ling _____
4. ping-siunn _____
5. mi̍h(-kiānn) _____
6. puànn-mê-á _____
7. khui _____
8. pak-tóo-iau _____
9. kan-na _____
10. í-king _____

(a) milk (from cows)
(b) in the middle of the night
(c) only, merely, no more than
(d) (material) things; object, item
(e) to be hungry
(f) fridge, freezer
(g) to search, to look for
(h) already
(i) to spoil (food), to go sour
(j) to open; to be open; to turn on

E02 Fill in the blanks with one of the words you've learned in this lesson.

1. (_____) lāi-té ū gōo lia̍p suāinn-á.
   There are five mangoes in the fridge.

2. Ông--sian-sinn (_____) pài-la̍k tsiah ū-îng.
   Mr. Ong is available only on Saturdays.

3. Guá kah a-má beh khì tshī-tiûnn bé (_____).
   Grandma and I are going to the market to do some shopping.

4. Toh-tíng hit pue si-kue-tsiap (_____)--ah.
   That glass of watermelon juice on the table has gone sour.

5. I-sing kiò lí m̄-thang iōng (_____) tshī niau-á.
   The doctor told you not to feed cow's milk to the cat.

I was hungry in the middle of the night.

LESSON 17

6. Tshù-lāi ū-kàu juảh! Lí khì (   ) thang-á, hó--bô?
   It's terribly hot in the house! Go open the windows, would you?

7. I thâu-tú-á tsiah tsiảh-pá, tsit-má iū-koh (   )--ah!
   She was full just a while ago, and now she's hungry again!

8. Guá ê tshiú-ki-á m̄ tsai tsáu khì tó-uī, sì-kè lóng (   ) bô.
   I wonder where my cell phone has gone; I can't find it anywhere.

9. Lí sàng ê lé-bu̍t, guá (   ) siu--tio̍h--ah.
   I have already received the gift you sent me.

10. Tsuè-kīn a-kong tiānn-tiānn (   ) tshut-khì sàn-pōo.
    Lately, grandpa has frequently gone out to take a stroll in the middle of the night.

E03 Translate the sentences into English.

1. Guá tsin tshuì-ta, tsia kám ū tsuí thang lim?

   _____.

2. Hit king tiàm sing-lí tsiok bái, í-king kuainn tiàm--ah.

   _____.

E04 Can you figure out how to say…?

Take a look at the vocabulary list and see if you can figure out how to say these sentences in Taiwanese:

1. "The rice milk smells really good!"
2. "I'd like two cups of iced soy milk."

Listen to **Audio 17-4** and see how you did!

SHORT TAKES

LESSON 18

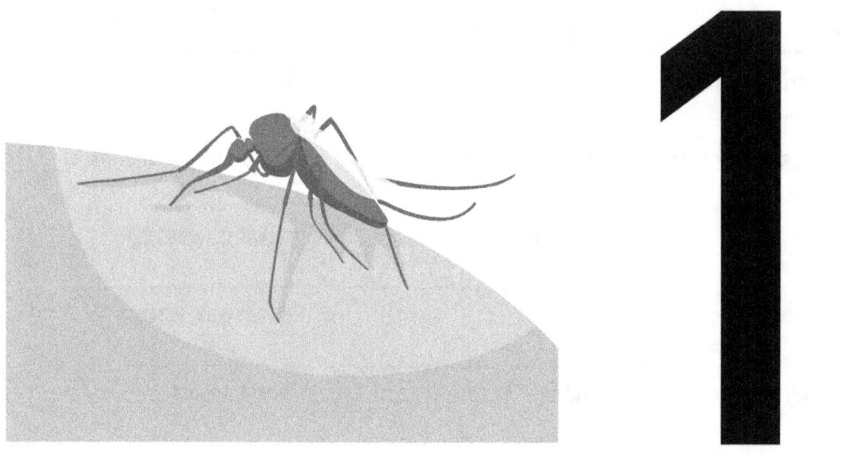

There are so many mosquitoes in the house!

Picture the short scene described in English below, and then try to associate the underlined words with the Taiwanese translation.

🎧 Audio 18-1

There were so <u>many</u>   <u>mosquitoes</u> in the house.
            kāu   báng

They <u>kept</u>   <u>bothering</u> and <u>stinging me</u>,
    tit-tit tshá   kā guá tìng

<u>making</u> me <u>unable to sleep</u> the whole night,
hāi   bē khùn--tit

and also <u>tired</u>   <u>at work</u> the next day.
       bô tsing-sîn siōng-pan

VOCABULARY | Gí-sû 語詞

Audio 18-2

WORD	MEANING	RELATED WORDS	MEANING
kāu 厚	thick, dense; strong, concentrated; numerous, abundant	Tsiú tsiok kāu. 酒足厚。	The liquor is very strong.
		Tsheh tsin kāu. 冊真厚。	The book is really thick.
		kāu-uē 厚話	talkative; gossipy
		po̍h 薄	thin; weak, watery
báng(-á) 蠓(仔)	mosquito	thâng 蟲	worm; insect
		káu-hiā 狗蟻	ant
		ka-tsua̍h 虼蚻	cockroach
		phang 蜂	bee, wasp
ti̍t-ti̍t 直直	constantly; directly; squarely; straight on	it-ti̍t 一直	constantly; straight on
		ti̍t 直	straight, upright; direct, blunt
tshá 吵	noisy; to make a noise, to quarrel, to bother	tiām 恬	quiet, silent
		tiām-tiām 恬恬	Be quiet! (as an order); quietly, silently

There are so many mosquitoes in the house!

WORD	MEANING	RELATED WORDS	MEANING
kā guá tìng 共 我 叮	to sting me, to bite me	kā 共	for, on behalf of, to, at, from (*object marker* in the disposal construction)
		subj. + kā + *obj.* + *verb*	
		subj. + kā + *obj.* + *verb phrase (disposal)*	
		kā lâng kóng 共 人 講	to tell people/others
		kā guá phah 共 我 拍	to hit me
		kā i bé 共 伊 買	to buy from him; to buy for him
		kā mn̂g khui--khui 共 門 開開	to make the door open, to open the door
		tìng 叮	to sting (insect)
hāi 害	to harm; to cause/make *sb* to (do something against one's will); to be damaged/broken, to go bad or spoil	hāi--lâng 害 人	to do harm to people, to be harmful
		hāi--khì 害 去	to go bad or spoil; to be broken
		Hāi--ah! 害 矣！	Oh, shoot! We're in deep trouble; I'm screwed/done for
		Tsin hāi! 真 害！	Goodness! What a mess!

WORD	MEANING	RELATED WORDS	MEANING
khùn 睏	to sleep	khùn--khì 睏去	to fall asleep
		khùn-tàu 睏晝	to take a nap after lunch
		hioh-khùn 歇睏	to rest, to take a rest
		hioh-khùn-jit / hioh-khùn-lit 歇睏日	holiday
		ài-khùn 愛睏	sleepy
bē-tit / buē-tit 袂得	to be unable/ impossible to (usu. because the circumstances don't allow) **bē-tit** + *verb* **bē** + *verb* + **--tit** (un-*verb*-able)	ē-tit 會得 **ē-tit** + *verb* **ē** + *verb* + **--tit**	to be able/possible to
		bē tsia̍h--tit / buē tsia̍h--eh 袂食得	to be inedible
		bē-kì--tit / buē-kì--eh 袂記得	to forget, to be unable to remember
		ē-īng--tit / ē-īng--eh 會用得	to be usable/doable; to be suitable
		bē-īng--tit / buē-īng--eh 袂用得	to be unusable/unworkable; to be unsuitable
		ē-tàng / ē-tit-thang 會當 / 會得通	can, to be able to, to get to do *sth*
		bē-tàng / bē-tit-thang 袂當 / 袂得通	cannot, to be able to, to not get to do *sth*

There are so many mosquitoes in the house!

LESSON 18

WORD	MEANING	RELATED WORDS	MEANING
bô tsing-sîn 無精神	without energy, tired, bushed	tsing-sîn 精神	spirit, mind, energy; to wake up (from sleep)
		tshénn / tshínn 醒	to become awake or sober; to regain consciousness
		thiám 忝	tired, exhausted; severe, thorough
siōng-pan 上班	to go to work; at work	hā-pan 下班	to get off work/duty
		siōng-khò 上課	to go to class; at school
		hā-khò 下課	to get out of class, to finish class

SHORT TAKES

REVIEW | Ho̍k-sip 復習

Listen to **Audio 18-3** and read the story in Taiwanese.

Tshù-lāi báng tsiok kāu,
厝內 蠓 足 厚,

Tit-tit lâi kā guá tshá, kā guá tìng,
直直 來 共 我 吵、共 我 叮,

hāi guá kui-mê bē khùn--tit,
害 我 規暝 袂 睏得,

siōng-pan mā bô tsing-sîn.
上班 嘛 無 精神。

Translation

There were so many mosquitoes in the house.
They kept bothering and stinging me,
making me unable to sleep the whole night,
and also tired at work the next day.

DID YOU KNOW... | Lí kám tsai-iánn... 你敢知影...

Besides the sweltering heat of the Taiwanese summers, **báng-á** 蠓仔 (mosquitoes) can also be a force to reckon with! Their incessant buzzing can keep you awake at night, and if you let your guard down, you may suddenly find yourself with a collection of itchy, red bites. To survive the summer, most Taiwanese households have specialized equipment on hand to defend against the onslaught, from the more old-fashioned **báng-á-hiunn** 蠓仔香 (mosquito repellent coils or incense) and **báng-tà** 蠓罩 (mosquito nets) to the more "deadly" **báng-phia̍k-á** 蠓擗仔, also called **tiān-báng-sut-á** 電蠓捽仔 (electric swatters), and fluorescent blue **báng-á-ting** 蠓仔燈 (bug zappers). Some mosquitoes in Taiwan have been found to spread **thian-káu-jia̍t** 天狗熱 (dengue fever) and **Ji̍t-pún náu-iām** 日本腦炎 (Japanese encephalitis), so be sure to protect yourself!

Another notorious pest known to locals is the tiny fly known as **oo-bui-á** 烏蝛仔 (midges or "no-see-ums"). These little beasts even have the word "Taiwan" in their scientific name: *Forcipomyia taiwana*. While the midges are tiny, black, and typically only around 1/25 inch (1 mm), their bites can cause an outsized terrible, itchy rash (or a more serious allergic reaction) that some find worse than mosquito bites. These midges are typically found around mossy areas such as gardens, bamboo groves, and near the corners between walls. They are most active from late morning to early afternoon during the warmer months. Wearing long-sleeve clothes, long pants, and insect repellent can go a long way in helping to protect yourself from their bites.

EXERCISES | Liān-sı̇p 練習

E01 Match each Taiwanese word to its English translation.

1. báng   ____   (a) mosquito
2. siōng-pan   ____   (b) to sting me
3. hāi   ____   (c) constantly; straight
4. tshá   ____   (d) noisy; to make a noise, to bother
5. kā guá tìng   ____   (e) to be unable/impossible to
6. bô tsing-sîn   ____   (f) without energy, tired
7. tı̇t-tı̇t   ____   (g) to go to work; at work
8. kāu   ____   (h) to harm; to cause *sb.* to; to go bad
9. khùn   ____   (i) to sleep
10. bē-tit   ____   (j) thick; strong; numerous

E02 Fill in the blanks with one of the words you've learned in this lesson.

1. Tâi-pak (   ) lo̍h-hōo.
   It keeps raining in Taipei.

2. Guā-kháu siunn (   ), lán lâi-khì lāi-té kóng.
   It's too noisy outside; let's go inside to talk.

3. I ê kha khì hōo (   ) tìng--tio̍h.
   His leg got bitten by a mosquito.

4. Guá ê tshiú-ki-á hōo guán pîng-iú sńg kah (   )--khì.
   My cell phone got damaged because my friend messed around with it.

5. Guán sió-muē tiānn-tiānn khiâ oo-tóo-bái (   ).
   My sister often goes to work by scooter.

6. Hit kuàn gû-ling tshàu-sng--khì, (   )-lim-(   )--ah!
   That bottle of milk has gone sour and has become/is now undrinkable.

There are so many mosquitoes in the house!

7. Tân thài-**thài** siu-tio̍h hit tiunn **phue**, huân-ló kah bē **tsia̍h** bē (   )--tit.
   Having received that letter, Mrs. Tan got so worried that she couldn't eat or sleep.

8. Kin-á-**ji̍t** tsiânn **kuânn**, ài tshīng tsi̍t niá (   ) ê phòng-se-**sann**, tsiah bē **kuânn**--tio̍h.
   It's really cold today. You should wear a heavy sweater so you won't catch a cold.

E03 Put the words in the right order to make a sentence.

1. lóng / ē / that / in / kha-kiû / khì / hioh-khùn-ji̍t
   (Every holiday they would go play soccer.)

   _____.

2. tō / guá / nā / liâm-mi / siá--lo̍h-lâi / bē-kì--tit / bô
   (If I don't write it down, I will forget it right away.)

   _____.

3. bô tsing-sîn / tsa-mê / bô / guá / siōng-khò / tsiok / tsái-khí / khùn
   (I didn't sleep last night, so I am so tired in class this morning.)

   _____.

4. bē-kì-tit / i / ti̍t-ti̍t / kóng / tshá / guá / siánn / beh / hāi
   (She kept making noises, which made me forget what I wanted to say.)

   _____.

E04 Can you figure out how to say…?

Take a look at the vocabulary list and see if you can figure out how to say these sentences in Taiwanese:

1. "He has woken up."
2. "Sorry, I can't tell you."

Listen to **Audio 18-4** and see how you did!

LESSON 19

The bathroom light was broken.

Picture the short scene described in English below, and then try to associate the underlined words with the Taiwanese translation.

🎧 Audio 19-1

The <u>bathroom</u>   <u>light</u>   was <u>broken</u>,
　　piān-sóo　　tiān-hué　　pháinn--khì

so it was <u>pitch black</u>   inside.
　　　　àm-bîn-bong

He <u>thought of</u> the <u>ghost flick</u> he had watched
　　siūnn--tio̍h　　　kuí-á-phinn

the night before, and got so <u>scared</u> he didn't
　　　　　　　　　　　　　　kiann

even <u>dare</u>   <u>go in</u>   to <u>pee</u>.
　　　kánn　ji̍p--khì　　pàng-jiō

166

VOCABULARY | Gí-sû 語詞

 Audio 19-2

WORD	MEANING	RELATED WORDS	MEANING
piān-sóo 便所	restroom, toilet	ik-king-á 浴間仔	bathroom, shower room
		pâng-king 房間	room (in a house)
		tsàu-kha / tû-pâng 灶跤 / 廚房	kitchen
		kheh-thiann 客廳	living room
tiān-hué / tiān-hé 電火	electric light, lamp	tsit pha tiān-hué / tsit pha tiān-hé 一 葩 電火	a light, a lamp ("pha": *measure word* for lamps, a bunch of flowers, a bunch of grapes)
		tiān 電	electricity, electric
		hué / hé 火	fire
		huan-á-hué / huan-á-hé 番仔火	match (for lighting fire)
		lài-tah （ライター）	lighter
pháinn--khì 歹去	to be broken, out of order; to go bad, rotten	--khì 去	(*verbal complement*) gone, away
		bô--khì 無去	to be gone, to disappear
		phuà--khì 破去	to be broken, to be worn-out/ripped
		khì--ah 去 矣	It's gone; gone (died); We're doomed!

SHORT TAKES

WORD	MEANING	RELATED WORDS	MEANING
àm-bîn-bong / àm-mi-moo 暗眠摸	to be pitch black, to be very dark	àm 暗	dark; late; night
		kng 光	bright, shiny; light
siūnn--tio̍h 想著	to think of, to call to mind	siūnn 想	to think
		siūnn-kóng 想講	to think that, to consider that
kuí-á-phìnn 鬼仔片	ghost flick, ghost movie	kuí 鬼	ghost, spirit
		sîn 神	god, spirit
		iánn-phìnn 影片	movie, video (clip)
kiann 驚	scared, afraid (of); to scare	heh-kiann / hennh-kiann 嚇驚	to scare
		kā + *sb* + **heh-kiann**	to scare *sb*
		kiann-á / kiann-eh 驚了 / 驚見	to be afraid that, to fear that
		khióng-pòo 恐怖	terrifying, scary, horrible
kánn 敢	dare; bold	m̄ kánn 毋敢	dare not, to not have the courage/guts
		bô-tánn 無膽	cowardly, gutless, wimpy

The bathroom light was broken.

LESSON 19

WORD	MEANING	RELATED WORDS	MEANING
ji̍p--khì / li̍p--khì 入去	to get in, to go in; in (*directional complement*)	ji̍p / li̍p 入	to put in, to go in; in
		ji̍p--lâi / li̍p--lâi 入來	to come in; in (*directional complement*)
		tshut 出	to exit, to go out; to occur; to publish
		tshut--khì 出去	to get out, to go out; out (*directional complement*)
		tshut--lâi 出來	to come out; out (*directional complement*)
pàng-jiō / pàng-liō 放尿	to pee, to urinate	pàng-sái 放屎	to poop, to defecate
		Pháinn-sè, guá beh lâi piān-sóo--tsi̍t-ē. 歹勢，我 欲 來去 便所 一下。	Excuse me, I need to use the restroom. I'll be right back.

SHORT TAKES

REVIEW | Ho̍k-si̍p 復習

Listen to Audio **19-3** and read the story in Taiwanese.

Piān-sóo ê tiān-hué pháinn--khì,
便所 的 電火 歹去,

Kui lāi-té àm-bîn-bong.
規 內底 暗眠摸。

I siūnn-tio̍h tsa-mê khuànn ê kuí-á-phìnn,
伊 想著 昨暝 看 的 鬼仔片,

Kiann kah m̄ kánn ji̍p-khì pàng-jiō.
驚 甲 毋 敢 入去 放尿。

Translation

The bathroom light was broken,

so it was pitch black inside.

He thought of the ghost flick he had watched the night before,

and got so scared he didn't even dare go in to pee.

The bathroom light was broken.

DID YOU KNOW… | Lí kám tsai-iánn… 你敢知影…

The major religions in Taiwan are **Hu̍t-kàu** / **Pu̍t-kàu** 佛教 (Buddisim) and **Tō-kàu** 道教 (Taoism), which are mixed with elements of **Jû-kàu** / **Khóng-tsú-kàu** 儒教 / 孔子教 (Confucianism) and traditional folk beliefs. All together they account for about 60–70% of the population. Some folk beliefs originally came from the indigenous (Formosan-Austronesian) cultures or were brought over by early immigrants from the Southern Fujian and Guangdong regions in China, while others originated in Taiwan from unknown sources or in unknown periods.

Here are a few common folk beliefs and superstitions concerning ghosts:

1) Never stick your chopsticks in the rice. Not only is it considered rude in Taiwan, but it also resembles the **kha-bué-png** 跤尾飯, which is a bowl of rice placed beside the feet of a dead person at a funeral.

2) During "Ghost Month" (the 7th month of the traditional calendar), there are many things one should not do. For instance, do not whistle or hang your clothes outside at night because this will attract ghosts, or the so-called **hó-hiann-tī** 好兄弟 (literally "good brothers"), a euphemism for those who have died from a tragic or unexpected cause, were unburied and forgotten, and then became wandering ghosts.

3) Many people will burn **gîn-tsuá** 銀紙 ("silver-paper", paper money for the dead), paper houses, paper cars, and so on as a way to send them to be used by ancestors and people in the netherworld.

SHORT TAKES

EXERCISES | Liān-si̍p 練習

E01 Match each Taiwanese word to its English translation.

1. àm-bîn-bong ____
2. piān-sóo ____
3. pàng-jiō ____
4. tiān-hué ____
5. kuí-á-phìnn ____
6. kiann ____
7. kánn ____
8. ji̍p--khì ____
9. pháinn--khì ____
10. siūnn--tio̍h ____

(a) to pee, to urinate
(b) restroom, toilet
(c) to get in, to go in; in
(d) scared, afraid (of); to scare
(e) to think of, to call to mind
(f) to be broken; to go bad, rotten
(g) dare; bold
(h) to be pitch black
(i) electric light, lamp
(j) ghost flick, ghost movie

E02 Fill in the blanks with one of the words you've learned in this lesson.

1. I siūnn-beh (_____), suah tshuē-bô (_____).
   He wants to pee, but he can't find a toilet.

2. Tshù-lāi (_____), guá lâi-khì khui (_____).
   It's so dark in the house; I'll go turn the lights on.

3. (_____) āu kò gue̍h beh khì Ji̍t-pún, guá tō tsiok huann-hí.
   Just thinking that I'm going to Japan next month already makes me so happy.

4. Tsiânn hāi! Guá ê tiān-náu kánn-ná (_____)--ah!
   Oh no! My computer seems to be broken!

5. I ê lú pîng-iú tsin ài khuànn tiān-iánn, liân (_____) mā tsiok ài khuànn.
   Her girlfriend really likes to watch movies—even ghost movies she really loves to watch.

The bathroom light was broken.

6. Lín sī-án-tsuánn m̄ (   ) kah i kóng-uē?
   Why are you afraid of talking to her?

7. I beh (   ) pâng-king hioh-khùn--ah.
   He's going into the room to rest.

8. Pâng-king-lāi ū ka-tsuah, hāi i (   ) kah khùn-bē-khì.
   There's a cockroach in the room, which makes him so scared that he can't fall asleep.

E03 Translate the sentences into English..

1. Guá siánn-mih lóng m̄ kiann!

   _____.

2. Pháinn-sè, tshiánn-mn̄g piān-sóo tī tó-uī?

   _____.

E04 Can you figure out how to say...?

Take a look at the vocabulary list and see if you can figure out how to say these sentences in Taiwanese:

1. "He's afraid of ghosts."
2. "My lighter is gone."
3. "That video is really terrifying. I don't dare to watch it."

Listen to Audio 19-4 and see how you did!

LESSON 20

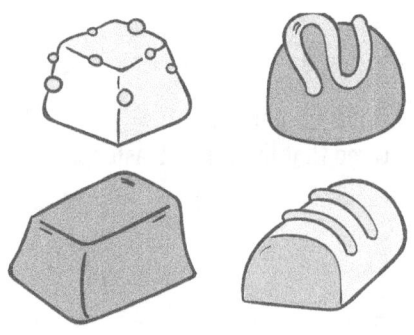

Picture the short scene described in English below, and then try to associate the underlined words with the Taiwanese translation.

 Audio 20-1

<u>Uncle</u> always <u>brings</u> us a <u>box</u> of
a-tsik　　　　　theh　　　　ah

<u>Swiss</u>　<u>chocolates</u>　<u>whenever</u> he visits.
Suī-sū　tsio-kóo-lè-toh　ê sî

He said <u>life</u>　　is full of hard times,
　　　　tsit-si-lâng

<u>so</u>　　we should enjoy <u>some</u>　<u>sweetness</u>.
sóo-í　　　　　　　　tsit-kuá　tinn

VOCABULARY | Gí-sû 語詞

 Audio 20-2

WORD	MEANING	RELATED WORDS	MEANING
a-tsik 阿叔	father's younger brother (uncle)	a-tsím 阿嬸	wife of father's younger brother (aunt)
		a-peh 阿伯	father's older brother (uncle)
		a-ḿ 阿姆	wife of father's older brother (aunt)
		a-kū 阿舅	mother's brother
		a-kīm 阿妗	wife of mother's brother
the̍h 提	to take, to get, to hold	khǹg 囥	to put; to put aside
		khǹg--lo̍h 囥落	to put down
a̍h / a̍p 盒	box (of)	a̍h-á / a̍p-á 盒仔	box
		kheh-á 篋仔	box, case (usu. small, drawer-like, with or without a lid)
		siunn-á 箱仔	chest, large box
Suī-sū 瑞士	Switzerland	Suī-tián 瑞典	Sweden
		Se-pan-gâ 西班牙	Spain
		Hô-lân / Hô-lan 荷蘭	Holland; the Netherlands

SHORT TAKES

WORD	MEANING	RELATED WORDS	MEANING
tsio-kóo-lè-toh (チョコレート)	chocolate	thn̂g-á 糖仔	candy
		thn̂g 糖	sugar
		piánn 餅	cookie, cracker, cake (generic term for round flat pastries)
		thn̂g-á-piánn 糖仔餅	candies and cookies, sweets
ê sî(-tsūn) 的 時(陣)	when, at/during the time that, while … + ê sî	sî-kan 時間	time, hours (for doing *sth*); clock time
		ū-sî(-á) 有時(仔)	sometimes
		tang-sî / tī-sî 當時 / 底時	when (in a question)
		kuí tiám 幾 點	what time (o'clock)
tsi̍t-sì-lâng 一世人	a lifetime; all one's life	tsit-sì-lâng 這世人	this life, this lifetime
		tshut-sì 出世	to be born
		jîn-sing / lîn-sing 人生	life, human life
só͘-í 所以	therefore, so	in-uī 因為	because
(tsi̍t-)kuá (一)寡	some, a few	sió-khuá-á 小可仔	a little, a bit; slightly
		kuí 幾	several, a couple of
		Kuí ê? 幾 个?	How many? (usu. countable and small number)

Uncle always brings us a box of Swiss chocolates.

LESSON 20

WORD	MEANING	RELATED WORDS	MEANING
tinn 甜	sweet, sugary	kam 甘	sweet (aftertaste), umami
		khóo 苦	bitter; tough
		bī 味	taste, smell, flavor

REVIEW | Ho̍k-si̍p 復習

Listen to Audio 20-2 and read the story in Taiwanese.

A-tsik ta̍k-pái lâi ê sî,
阿叔 逐 擺 來 的 時,

lóng ē the̍h tsi̍t a̍h Suī-sū tsio-kóo-lè-toh lâi sàng--guán.
攏 會 提 一 盒 瑞士 tsio-kóo-lè-toh 來 送 阮。

I kóng tsi̍t-sì-lâng hiah-nī kan-khóo,
伊 講 一世人 遐爾 艱苦,

Sóo-í tio̍h-ài tsia̍h tsi̍t-kuá tinn--ê.
所以 著愛 食 一寡 甜的。

Translation

Uncle always brings us a box of Swiss chocolates whenever he visits.

He said life is full of hard times,

so we should enjoy some sweetness.

DID YOU KNOW… | Lí kám tsai-iánn… 你敢知影…

Kinship terms and the ways to address people are a little complex in Taiwanese, but you may have noticed some rules from the words we have already learned. Here are both some linguistic and cultural tips:

"**-m**" is the female counterpart of some kinship terms, so the wife of **kū** 舅 is **kīm** 妗, the wife of **tsik** 叔 is **tsím** 嬸, and the wife of **peh** 伯 is **ḿ** 姆.

Adding the prefix "**a-**" is a common way to form terms of endearment. There are a few examples we have come across in this lesson (e.g. **a-tsik** 阿叔, **a-peh** 阿伯) and also in earlier lessons like **a-kong** 阿公 (grandpa) and **a-má** 阿媽 (grandma). In fact, another way to say "dad" and "mom" is **a-pah** 阿爸 and **a-bú** 阿母. While these "**a-**" words are normally used when addressing that person directly, you can also use these terms when referring to them indirectly with other people.

This pattern of creating terms of endearment can also apply to given names. Many nicknames are formed by taking out a syllable from someone's given name and adding the prefix "**A-**" (e.g. **A-tsì** 阿志), or a diminutive suffix "**--á**" (e.g. **tîng--á** 庭仔), or even both (e.g. **A-iông--á** 阿揚仔). It's similar to how we sometimes modify names in English: Katherine > Katie, Matthew > Matt or Matty, Stephen > Stevie.

However, familiarity sometimes breeds contempt, so beware that some of the terms derived from diminutive structures can also sound a little jokey and therefore might have a slightly derogatory connotation. For example, **a-tok-á** 阿啄仔 is a white person or a Westerner, originally meaning "someone with a pointy, beak-like nose", or "**a-pún-á** 阿本仔", meaning someone from Japan (**Jit-pún** 日本). Depending on the context, these words may be used to show either friendliness or contempt.

EXERCISES | Liān-si̍p 練習

E01 Match each Taiwanese word to its English translation.

1. tinn _____ (a) box (of)
2. tsio-kóo-lè-toh _____ (b) chocolate
3. a-tsik _____ (c) therefore, so
4. ê sî(-tsūn) _____ (d) sweet, sugary
5. tsit-kuá _____ (e) father's younger brother (uncle)
6. tsit-sì-lâng _____ (f) to take, to get, to hold
7. sóo-í _____ (g) some, a few
8. Suī-sū _____ (h) when, at/during the time that
9. the̍h _____ (i) Switzerland
10. a̍h _____ (j) a lifetime; all one's life

E02 Fill in the blanks with one of the words you've learned in this lesson.

1. Tsit lia̍p liú-ting tsiânn ( ).
   This orange is really sweet.

2. ( ), lí tang-sî beh koh khì Ho-lan?
   Uncle (father's younger brother), when are you going to Holland again?

3. Toh-tíng hit ( ) thn̂g-á senn tsiok tsē káu-hiā.
   The box of candies on the table attracted so many ants.

4. Guá khǹg tī kheh-thiann ê kheh-á, siánn-lâng ( )--khì?
   Who took away the box I put in the living room?

5. Guá siūnn-kóng lín í-king tsai--ah, ( ) bô kā lín kóng.
   I thought you already knew, so I didn't tell you.

Uncle always brings us a box of Swiss chocolates.

6. Hā-pan (   ), lán lâi-khì tsia̍h suāinn-á-ping!
   Let's go eat mango shaved ice after work!

7. In āu-pái beh tsò-hué khì (   ) peh suann.
   They are going to go hiking together in Switzerland next time.

8. Tsit ê (   ) sī-án-tsuánn tsiah-nī khóo?
   Why is this chocolate so bitter?

9. Tsò lāu-pē lāu-bú--ê, (   ) huân-ló gín-á.
   Being a parent, you're going to worry about your children all of your life.

E03 Put the words in the right order to make a sentence.

1. beh / ū / tsit-kuá / tsàu-kha / lí / bí-hún / tsia̍h / kám
   (There are rice noodles in the kitchen; do you want to eat some?)

   _____.

2. sńg / ê / tsia̍h-pn̄g / sî-tsūn / tshiú-ki-á / m̄-thang
   (Don't play on your phone while you are eating.)

   _____.

E04 Can you figure out how to say...?

Take a look at the vocabulary list and see if you can figure out how to say these sentences in Taiwanese:

1. "Sorry, I don't have time."
2. "What time is it now?"
3. "My mother's brother was born in Spain."

Listen to **Audio 20-3** and see how you did!

SHORT TAKES

ANSWER KEY | Huê-tap 回答

LESSON 01

Main Dialogue with Tone Markings

Kin⁷-á¹-**jit** tsiok⁸ **jua̍h!**

Guá¹ e⁷-**poo** beh²⁻¹ khì²⁻¹ siû⁷-**tsuí.**

Guá¹ ê⁷ **káu** mā³ beh²⁻¹ khì²⁻¹ **siû.**

E01   d, g, e, a, j, f, i, h, b, c

E02

1. (Kin⁷-á¹-**jit**) tsiok⁸ **kuânn!**
   It's so cold <u>today</u>!

2. Guá¹ e⁷-**poo** beh²⁻¹ khì²⁻¹ (siû⁷-**tsuí**).
   I want to go <u>swimming</u> this afternoon.

3. Guá¹ ê⁷ (**káu**) mā³ beh²⁻¹ khì²⁻¹ **siû.**
   My <u>dog</u> also wants to go swimming.

4. Tsit⁸-**má** (tsiok⁸ / tsiânn⁷ / tsin⁷) **jua̍h.**
   It's <u>so</u> hot now.

5. Guán¹ (mā³) siūnn³-beh²⁻¹ **khì.**
   We would like to go, <u>too</u>.

E03 Audio:

1. Guá¹ tsit⁸-**má** beh²⁻¹ khì²⁻¹ siû⁷-**tsuí.**
   I'm going to swim now.

2. Tsái¹-**khí** tsiok⁸ **kuânn,** àm²-**sî** mā³ tsiok⁸ **kuânn.**
   It was cold in the morning. It was cold in the evening, too.

LESSON 02

Main Dialogue with Tone Markings

Guá¹ ū³ tsit⁴ ê⁷ pîng⁷-iú tuà² Bí¹-kok.

Guá¹ āu³ lé¹-**pài** beh²⁻¹ tsē³ hui⁷-ki khì.

Guá¹ tsah² tsiok⁸ tsē³ phàu²-**mī**!

E01   h, a, i, b, e, d, c, f, g, j

E02

1. Guá¹ (ū³) nñg³ ê⁷ pîng⁷-iú.
   I <u>have</u> two friends.

2. Guá¹ tsit⁸-**má** (tuà²) tī³ Bí¹-kok.
   I'm <u>living</u> in the US now.

3. Guá¹ kin⁷-â¹-**jit** beh²⁻¹ (tsē³) hui⁷-ki (khì²⁻¹) Jit⁴-pún.
   I'm <u>taking</u> a plane <u>to</u> Japan today

E03

1. Guá¹ ū³ tsiok⁸ tsē³ pîng⁷-iú.
   I have (so) many friends.

2. Lí¹ ê⁷ pîng⁷-iú āu³ lé¹-**pài** beh²⁻¹ khì²⁻¹ Bí¹-kok.
   Your friend is going to the US next week.

3. Guá¹ ū³ tsah² **tsînn**.
   I have brought (some) money. / I've got money in my pocket.

4. Lí¹ ū³ guā³-tsē³ phàu²-**mī**?
   How much instant ramen do you have?

E04 **Audio:**

1. Guá¹ ū³ nn̄g³ tsiah⁸ káu¹-**á**.
   I have two dogs.

2. Guá¹ bô⁷ pîng⁷-**iú**.
   I have no friends.

3. Guá¹ tuà² Ing⁷-**kok**. / Guá¹ tuà² tī³ Ing⁷-**kok**.
   I live in the UK.

LESSON 03

Main Dialogue with Tone Markings

I⁷ ē³-hiáu¹ kóng¹ Ing⁷-**gí**.

I⁷ ê⁷ lú¹ pîng⁷-**iú** sī³ Ing⁷-kok⁸-**lâng**.

I⁷ tiānn³-tiānn³ siá¹ **phue hōo**--i⁰.

E01   f, c, i, a, b, e, d, j, g, h

E02

1. Guá¹ ē³-hiáu¹ kóng¹ Tâi⁷-**gí**.
   I can speak Taiwanese.

2. I⁷ ê⁷ pîng⁷-**iú** sī³ Huat⁸-kok⁸-**lâng**.
   His/Her friend is French.

3. Guá¹ tiānn³-tiānn³ siá¹ **phue hōo**--in⁰.
   I often write letters to them.

4. I⁷ m̄³ sī³ guá¹ ê⁷ lâm⁷ pîng⁷-**iú**.
   He is not my boyfriend.

ANSWER KEY

E03
1. Guá¹ ê⁷ **káu** (ē³-hiáu¹) siû⁷-**tsuí**.
   My dog <u>knows how to</u> swim.

2. I⁷ (tiānn³-tiānn³) tsē³ hué¹-**tshia**.
   She takes trains <u>frequently</u>.

3. Guá¹ (siá¹) tsin⁷ tsē³ **phue**.
   I <u>wrote</u> many letters.

4. Guá¹ āu³ lé¹-**pài** ē³ siá¹ **phue** (hōo)--lí⁰.
   I will write a letter <u>to</u> you next week.

E04 **Audio:**

1. In⁷ bē³-hiáu¹ kóng¹ Ji̍t⁴-pún¹-**uē**. / In⁷ bē³-hiáu¹ kóng¹ Ji̍t⁴-**gí**.
   They can't speak Japanese.

2. Guá¹ hán¹-tit⁸ kóng¹ tiān³-**uē**.
   I seldom talk on the phone.

3. In⁷ kám¹-sī³ guā³-kok⁸-**lâng**? / In⁷ sī³-m̄³-sī³ guā³-kok⁸-**lâng**?
   Are they foreigners?

LESSON 04

Main Dialogue with Tone Markings

Guán¹ a⁷-**má** tuà² tī³ Tâi⁷-lâm⁷-**tshī**.

I⁷ ê⁷ **tshù** ū³ sann⁷ **lâu**.

I⁷ tshī³ la̍k⁴ tsiah² niau⁷-**á**, tsiok⁸ kóo¹-**tsui**!

E01   c, j, h, d, a, g, b, e, i, f

SHORT TAKES

E02

1. In⁷ ê⁷ **káu** mā³ tsin⁷ (kóo¹-**tsui**).
   Their dog is also very <u>cute</u>.

2. I⁷ kóng¹ i⁷ tiānn³-tiānn³ siá¹ **phue** hōo³ (a⁷-**má**).
   He says he often writes letters to <u>grandma</u>.

3. In⁷ lú¹ pîng⁷-iú ê⁷ **tshù** ū³ (la̍k⁴) tsàn² **lâu**.
   His girlfriend's house has <u>six</u> floors.

4. Guá¹ kin⁷-á¹-ji̍t tsē³ kè²-thîng⁷-**tshia** khì²⁻¹ (Tâi⁷-lâm⁷-**tshī**).
   I took a taxi to <u>Tainan City</u> today.

5. A⁷-**kong** (tī³) lâu⁷-**kha** leh²⁻¹ phàu² **tê**.
   Grandpa is making tea downstairs.

E03

1. Lín¹ a⁷-**kong** tshī³ sann⁷ tsiah² káu¹-**á**.
   Your grandpa raises/has three dogs.

2. Tshù²-**tíng** ū³ nn̄g³ tsiah² niau⁷-**á**.
   There are two cats on the roof.

3. Guán¹ tshù²-**pinn** sī³ Ko⁷-hiông⁷-**lâng**.
   My neighbor is from Kaohsiung ("Kaohsiung person").

4. A⁷-**má** hōo³ guán¹ tsi̍t⁴ tsiah² tsiok⁸ kóo¹-**tsui** ê⁷ niau⁷-**á**.
   Grandma gave us a very cute cat.

E04 **Audio:**

1. A⁷-**kong** ê⁷ **káu** tsiok⁸ kuai! / A⁷-**kong** ê⁷ **káu** tsin⁷ kuai!
   Grandpa's dog is really well-behaved.

2. Guá¹ tī³ **tshù**--lí⁰. / Guá¹ tī³ tshù²-**lāi**.
   I am at home.

ANSWER KEY

3. I⁷ tuà² sann⁷ hō jī³ lâu. / I⁷ tuà² tī³ sann⁷ hō jī³ lâu.
   She lives at no. 3, second floor.

LESSON 05

Main Dialogue with Tone Markings

Lán¹ lâi⁷-khì²⁻¹ se̍h³ iā³-**tshī**!

Iā³-**tshī lâng** tsiânn⁷ **tsē**, tsiânn⁷ lāu³-**jia̍t**!

Guá¹ beh²⁻¹ tsia̍h³ nn̄g³ uánn¹ lóo¹-bah²-**pn̄g**,

koh²⁻¹ lim⁷ tsi̍t⁴ pue⁷ si⁷-kue⁷-**tsiap**.

E01   i, f, b, a, h, d, j, g, c, e

E02
1. Guá¹ āu--ji̍t⁰ siūnn³-beh²⁻¹ (lâi⁷-khì²⁻¹) se̍h³ tshī³-tiûnn.
   I'd like to <u>go</u> to the market the day after tomorrow.

2. Kuânn⁷-thinn tshī³-tiûnn mā³ tsiânn⁷ (lāu³-jia̍t).
   The market is also very <u>busy</u> in the winter.

3. I⁷ kin⁷-á¹-ji̍t bô⁷ tsah² piān³-tong, (tsia̍h³) phàu²-mī.
   He didn't bring his lunchbox with him today. He's <u>eating</u> instant ramen.

4. Guá¹ hán¹-tit⁸ lâi⁷ (iā³-tshī).
   I rarely come to the <u>night market</u>.

5. A⁷-má bē³-hiáu¹ (lim⁷) tsiú.
   Grandma can't <u>drink</u>. / Grandma can't hold her liquor.

6. (Koh²⁻¹) lâi⁷ sann⁷ uánn¹ lóo¹-bah²-pn̄g.
   Three <u>more</u> bowls of braised pork rice, please.

SHORT TAKES

E03

1. Tâi⁷-**lâm** ū³ tsiok⁸ tsē³ iā³-**tshī**.
   (Tainan has many night markets.)

2. Guá¹ bô⁷ tsiảh³-**hun** mā³ bô⁷ lim⁷-**tsiú**.
   (I don't smoke and I don't drink.)

E04 **Audio:**

1. Guá¹ lim⁷ tsi̍t⁴ uánn¹ **thng**. / Guá¹ tsiảh³ tsi̍t⁴ uánn¹ **thng**.
   I had a bowl of soup.

2. Bí¹-**hún** tsiok⁸ hó¹ **tsiảh**!
   The rice noodles are so delicious!

3. Guá¹ beh²⁻¹ nňg³ pue⁷ liú¹-ting⁷-**tsiap**.
   I want two glasses of orange juice.

LESSON 06

Main Dialogue with Tone Markings

Lí¹ pài²-**it** ū³-**îng**--bô⁰?

Lán¹ lái⁹ khuànn² tiān³-**iánn, hó**--bô⁰?

Pháinn¹-**sè**, guá¹ tsuè²-**kīn** lâng bô⁷ sóng¹-**khuài**,

hit⁸ **kang** beh²⁻¹ khì²⁻¹ khuànn²-i⁷-**sing**.

E01   b, d, f, i, c, j, a, g, e, h

E02

Mon	Tue	Wed	Thu	Fri	Sat	Sun
pài²-**it**	pài²-**jī**	pài²-**sann**	pài²-**sì**	pài²-**gōo**	pài²-**lảk**	lé¹-**pài** / lé¹-**pài**²-**ji̍t**

ANSWER KEY

E03

1. Guá¹ (tsuè²-kīn) tiānn³-tiānn³ phuà²-pēnn.
   <u>Lately</u>, I have often been getting sick.

2. I⁷ ê⁷ lú¹ pîng⁷-iú lâng (bô⁷ sóng¹-khuài), tsit⁸-má leh²⁻¹ pēnn³-īnn.
   His girlfriend <u>is not feeling well</u>. She's in the hospital now.

3. A⁷-kong tī³ tshù²-lāi (khuànn²) tsheh.
   Grandpa <u>is reading</u> a book at home.

4. Pháinn¹-sè, lín¹ iáu¹-koh²⁻¹ ū³ king⁷-tsio--(bô⁰)?
   Excuse me, do you still have banana<u>s</u>?

5. Tsit⁸ ê⁷ ông⁷-lâi⁷-tsiap tsiânn⁷ (hó¹) lim.
   This pineapple juice tastes really <u>good</u>.

E04

1. Lán¹ pài²-sì lâi⁷-khì²⁻¹ Tâi⁷-pak, hó--bô⁰?
   How about going to Taipei with me on Thursday?

2. Guá¹ tsuè²-kīn tsin⁷ ū³-îng, khuànn² tsin⁷ tsē³ tshut⁸ tiān³-iánn.
   I've had so much time lately, (so) I watched a lot of movies.

3. Hit⁸ kang huān³-tsiá tsiok⁸ tsē, i⁷-sing tsiok⁸ bô⁷-îng.
   There were so many patients that day. The doctors were very busy.

E05 Audio:

1. Guá¹ tsit⁸ lé¹-pài ū³-îng.
   I am free this week.

2. Tsit⁸ tshut⁸ tiān³-iánn tsin⁷ hó¹-khuànn!
   This movie is good/interesting!

3. Lí¹ kīn³-lâi hó--bô⁰? / Lí¹ tsuè²-kīn hó--bô⁰?
   How have you been lately?

SHORT TAKES

LESSON 07

Main Dialogue with Tone Markings

Siòng²-phìnn lāi³-té hit⁸ ê⁷ sió¹-tsiá tsin⁷ suí!

Tshiánn¹-mn̄g i⁷ sī³ lín¹ sió¹-muē, iȧh³-sī³ lín¹ a⁷-tsí?

M̄³ sī³ guán¹ sió¹-muē, mā³ m̄³ sī³ guán¹ a⁷-tsí…

Sī³ guán¹ lāu³-bú--lah⁰!

E01   b, j, g, c, h, f, i, a, d, e

E02

1. Guán¹ pîng⁷-iú ê⁷ (sió¹-muē) tsiok⁸ kóo¹-tsui!
   My friend's <u>little sister</u> is so cute!

2. In⁷ (lāu³-bú) sī³ i⁷-sing.
   Her <u>mother</u> is a doctor.

3. Pháinn¹-sè, (tshiánn¹-mn̄g) lí¹ ū³ khuànn²-kìnn² guán¹ sió¹-tī--bô⁰?
   Excuse me, have you seen my little brother?

4. Kè²-thîng⁷-tshia⁷-lāi tsē³ tsi̍t⁴ ê⁷ (suí¹) koo⁷-niû.
   In the taxi sat a <u>beautiful</u> girl.

5. Guán¹ (a⁷-tsí) tshī ê⁷ káu tsin⁷ kuai.
   My <u>big sister</u>'s dog is really well-behaved.

6. Lín¹ ko--ko⁰ hit⁸ kang hip ê⁷ (siòng²-phìnn) tsin⁷ suí.
   The <u>pictures</u> that your big brother took that day are beautiful.

7. Tsit⁸ uánn¹ bí¹-hún¹-thng sī³ lí¹ ê (iȧh³-sī) guá¹ ê?
   Is this bowl of rice noodle soup yours <u>or</u> mine?

ANSWER KEY

8. Thài²-**thài**, guā³-**kháu** tsiok⁸ jua̍h, (lāi³-**té**) tshiánn¹-**tsē**--lah⁰.
   It's hot outside. Come on <u>in</u> and have a seat, ma'am.

E03 Audio:

1. Hit⁸ ê⁷ sian⁷-**sinn** m̄³ sī³ in⁷ lāu³-**pē**. / Hit⁸ ê⁷ sian⁷-**sinn** m̄³ sī³ in⁷ **pa**--pa⁰.
   That gentleman is not her father.

2. Sian⁷-**sinn**, tshiánn¹-**tsē**. / Sian⁷-**sinn**, lí¹ tshiánn¹-**tsē**.
   Please have a seat, sir.

3. Guā³-**kháu** ū³ tsi̍t⁴ ê⁷ siàu²-liân⁷-**lâng**. / Ū³ tsi̍t⁴ ê⁷ siàu²-liân⁷-**lâng** tī³ guā³-**kháu**.
   There's a young man outside.

LESSON 08

Main Dialogue with Tone Markings

I⁷ tsa⁷-**hng** khì²⁻¹ pah²-huè² kong⁷-**si**

bé¹ nn̄g³ niá¹ Sìng²-tàn² phòng²-se⁷-**sann**.

Sè² **niá**--ê⁰ sàng² in⁷ **bóo**,

tuā³ **niá**--ê⁰ ka⁷-**kī tshīng**.

E01   c, e, h, j, a, d, i, f, b, g

E02

1. Sit⁸-**lé**--lah⁰, guá¹ (tsa⁷-**hng**) tsiok⁸ bô⁷-**îng**.
   My apologies, I was so busy <u>yesterday</u>.

2. Guán¹ tshù²-**pinn** (sàng²) guán¹ tsin⁷ tsē³ suāinn⁷-**á**.
   Our neighbor <u>gave</u> us many mangoes.

3. In⁷ (**bóo**) tsuè²-kīn phuà²-pēnn, tsiah³ tsiok⁸ tsē³ ioh⁷-á.
His <u>wife</u> has been sick lately. She's taking a lot of medicine.

4. Kuânn⁷-thinn tsiânn⁷ tsē³ lâng (tshīng³) phòng²-se⁷-sann.
In the winter, many people <u>wear</u> sweaters.

5. Guá¹ pài²-gōo (**bé¹**) tsit⁴ kuàn² Huat⁸-kok⁸ **tsiú**, lí¹ beh²⁻¹ **lim--bô⁰**?
I <u>bought</u> a bottle of French wine on Friday. Do you want to drink it?

6. A⁷-tsí (**ka⁷-kī³**) tsit⁴ ê⁷ **lâng** tī³ lâu⁷-**tíng** leh²⁻¹ khuànn² tiān³-sī.
My big sister is watching TV upstairs all <u>by herself</u>.

7. Guá¹ beh²⁻¹ tsit⁴ pue⁷ (**tuā³**) **pue** ê⁷ phōng³-kó¹-tsiap.
I want a <u>large</u> glass of apple juice.

8. A⁷-**má** tshiah² tsit⁴ niá¹ (phòng²-se⁷-**sann**) hōo--guá⁰.
Grandma knitted me a <u>sweater</u>.

E03

1. I⁷ khì²⁻¹ kám¹-á¹-**tiàm** bé¹ lak⁴ kuàn² kué¹-tsí¹-**tsiap**.
(He went to the grocery store to buy six bottles of juice.)

2. Hit⁸ niá¹ khòo tsin⁷ sè² **niá**.
(That pair of pants is really small.)

3. In⁷ **ang** tī³ iā³-tshī⁷-á tsò²-sing⁷-lí.
(Her husband does business at the night market.)

4. Guá¹ tī³ Bí¹-kok tuā³-**hàn**.
(I grew up in the US.)

5. Lín¹ kóng¹-uē tsiânn⁷ tuā³-siann.
(You guys are talking really loudly.)

E04 **Audio:**

1. Tsîng⁷-jîn⁷-**tsiat** guá¹ sàng² i⁷ tsi̍t⁴ su⁷ **sann.** / Guá¹ Tsîng⁷-jîn⁷-**tsiat** sàng² i⁷ tsi̍t⁴ su⁷ **sann.**
   I gave her an entire outfit on Valentine's day.

2. Bîn⁷-á¹-**tsài** sī³ Kám¹-un⁷-**tsiat.** / Bîn⁷-á¹-**tsài** sī³ Kám¹-un⁷-**tseh.**
   Tomorrow is Thanksgiving.

LESSON 09

Main Dialogue with Tone Markings

Tsái¹-**khí** sī³ hó¹-**thinn,** ē⁷-**poo** suah² thàu²-**hong** lo̍h³-**hōo.**

Guá¹ tshut⁸-**mn̂g** bô⁷ tsah² hōo³-**suànn,**

Kui⁷-sin⁷-**khu** ak⁸ kah²⁻¹ tâm⁷-lok⁸-**lok!**

E01   e, a, i, f, c, j, b, h, d, g

E02
1. Bîn⁷-á¹-**tsài** sī³ (hó¹-**thinn**) a̍h³ pháinn¹-**thinn?**
   Is it a <u>sunny day</u> or a rainy day tomorrow?

2. In⁷ nn̄g³ ang⁷-á¹-**bóo** e⁷-**poo** beh²⁻¹ (tshut⁸-**mn̂g**) khuànn² tiān³-**iánn.**
   The couple is <u>going out</u> to see a movie this afternoon.

3. I⁷ tsa⁷-**hng** kóng¹ beh²⁻¹ **lâi,** kin⁷-á¹-**jit** (suah²) bô⁷ **lâi.**
   Yesterday he said he would come, <u>but actually</u> he didn't today.

4. Hōo³-lâi⁷-**thinn,** bē³ (hōo³-**suànn**) ê⁷ sing⁷-**lí** tsiok⁸ **hó.**
   On a rainy day, the <u>umbrella</u> seller's business is really good. / On a rainy day, umbrella sales are really good.

5. Lín¹ sió¹-**muē** tshīng³ (kah²⁻¹) suí¹-**tang**⁷-**tang.**
   Your little sister is dressed up so beautifully.

6. Guā³-kháu sī³ teh²⁻¹ (lo̍h³-hōo), sī--m̄⁰?
   Is it <u>raining</u> outside?

7. Guá¹ (kui⁷-sin⁷-khu) bô⁷ sóng¹-khuài.
   I hurt <u>all over</u>.

E03
1. I⁷ kui⁷-**kang** bô⁷ tshut⁸-mn̂g.
   He/She didn't go out for the whole day.

2. Guá¹ ū³ tsah² nn̄g³ ki⁷ hōo³-**suànn**, tsi̍t⁴ ki sàng--lí⁰.
   I brought two umbrellas. I'll give you one.

E04 **Audio:**

1. E⁷-**poo hong** tsin⁷ thàu.
   The wind was really strong in the afternoon.

2. Tsái¹-**khí** lo̍h³-hōo, guá¹ tshīng³ hōo³-mua tshut⁸-mn̂g.
   It was raining in the morning, so I went out in a raincoat.

3. Guá¹ tsái¹-**khí** tsia̍h³ kah²⁻¹ tsiok⁸ **pá**!
   I was so full this morning! (I got so full after breakfast!)

LESSON 10

Main Dialogue with Tone Markings

Lín¹ **tau** ū³-**kàu²** hn̄g!

Guá¹ kiânn⁷ nn̄g³ tiám¹-**tsing** tsiah²⁻¹ **kàu²**-uī,

Āu³-**pái** bô⁷ ài² **lâi**--ah⁰!

E01   e, h, j, a, c, g, i, b, f, d

ANSWER KEY

E02

1. Guá¹ (bô⁷ ài²) kiânn⁷-lōo, guá¹ beh²⁻¹ tsē³ kong⁷-tshia.
   I <u>don't feel like</u> walking. I'm going to take a bus.

2. (Lín¹ tau) tuà² toh?
   Where do you live? / Where is <u>your place</u>?

3. Guán¹ lú¹ pîng⁷-iú ê⁷ kong⁷-si tsiânn⁷ (hng).
   My girlfriend's company is really <u>far</u>.

4. Tse lóo¹-bah²-pn̄g (ū³-kàu²) hó¹-tsiah, guá¹ koh²⁻¹ beh²⁻¹ tsit⁴ uánn!
   This braised pork rice is <u>so</u> tasty. I want another bowl of it!

5. In⁷ sió¹-tī āu³ kò² gueh (tsiah²⁻¹) beh²⁻¹ tshut⁸-kok.
   His little brother <u>isn't</u> going abroad <u>until</u> next month.

6. Tsē³ hui⁷-ki khì²⁻¹ Jit⁴-pún ài² sann⁷ (tiám¹-tsing).
   It takes three <u>hours</u> to fly to Japan.

7. Lán¹ (āu³-pái) tsiah²⁻¹ koh²⁻¹ kóng.
   Let's talk about it <u>next time</u>. / Let's keep it for <u>next time</u>.

8. A⁷-kong tshī ê⁷ niau⁷-á tī³ tshù²-lāi (kiânn⁷) lâi (kiânn⁷) khì.
   Grandpa's cat is <u>walking</u> to and fro in the house.

E03

1. Hit⁸ tiunn⁷ phue, lí¹ (ài²) ka⁷-kī siá.
   That letter, you need to write yourself.

2. Lín¹ āu--jit⁰ kám¹ (ē³) lâi⁷ guán¹ tau?
   Will you come to my place the day after tomorrow?

3. Guán¹ ko--ko⁰ (ē³-hiáu¹) tshiah²-phòng²-se.
   My big brother knows how to knit.

4. Kin⁷-á¹-jit (bē³) loh³-hōo.
   It won't rain today.

SHORT TAKES

5. I⁷ (bô⁷ ài²) tsiȧh³ ioh⁷-**á**.
   He doesn't want to take medicine.

6. Hit⁸ ê⁷ siàu²-liân⁷-**lâng** (bē³-hiáu¹) tsò²-sing⁷-**lí**.
   That young man doesn't know how to do business.

E04 **Audio:**

1. Guán¹ tau tsiok⁸ kīn.
   My place is very close.

2. Guán¹ kàu²-**uī**--ah⁰.
   We have arrived.

3. Puànn² tiám¹-**tsing** bô⁷-**kàu**, ài² tsi̇t⁴ tiám¹-**tsing**.
   Half an hour is not enough. It needs an hour.

LESSON 11

Main Dialogue with Tone Markings

Tshiū⁷-á¹-**tíng** ū³ tsiáu¹-**á** teh²⁻¹ tshiùnn²-**kua**.

In⁷ kánn¹-ná¹ tsiok⁸ huann⁷-**hí**.

Guá¹ beh²⁻¹ peh²-khí¹-lì²⁻¹ kah²⁻¹ in⁷ tsò²-hué¹ **tshiùnn!**

E01   c, j, f, a, g, b, i, d, e, h

E02

1. Guán¹ lâm⁷ pîng⁷-**iú** bô⁷ ài² (kah²⁻¹) guá¹ khì²⁻¹ sėh³ pah²-huè² kong⁷-**si**.
   My boyfriend doesn't want to go shopping <u>with</u> me at the department store.

2. Lán¹ āu³-**pái** (tsò²-hué¹) khì²⁻¹ in⁷ tau tsiȧh³-**pn̄g**.
   Let's go to her place to have a meal <u>together</u> next time.

ANSWER KEY

3. Toh²-(**tíng**) ū³ tsit⁴ tiunn⁷ siōng²-**phìnn**.
   There's a photo <u>on</u> the table.

4. Guá¹ sàng² ti⁷-**ti** tsit⁴ ê⁷ hip⁸-siòng²-**ki**, i⁷ ū³-kàu² (**huann⁷-hí**)!
   I gave my little brother a camera. He was so <u>happy</u>!

5. A⁷-**má** tshī³ la̍k⁴ tsiah² niau⁷-**á**, nn̄g³ tsiah² (**tsiáu¹-á**).
   Grandma has six cats, two <u>birds</u>.

6. Guá¹ tuà² la̍k⁴ **lâu**, ài² (**peh²**) tsiok⁸ tsē³ lâu⁷-**thui**.
   I live on the sixth floor. I need to <u>climb</u> so many stairs.

7. (**Kánn¹-ná¹**) beh²⁻¹ lo̍h³-**hōo**--ah⁰. Lí¹ ū³ tsah² hōo³-**suànn**--bô⁰?
   <u>It seems like</u> it's going to rain now. Did you bring an umbrella?

8. Guá¹ bîn⁷-á¹-**tsài** ē³ tsē³ hué¹-**tshia** (**khí¹-lì²⁻¹**) Tâi⁷-**pak**.
   Tomorrow I will take a train to <u>go up to</u> Taipei.

E03

1. Tsit⁸ tsâng⁷ tshiū⁷-**á** tíng¹-**kuân** ū³ tsin⁷ tsē³ tshik⁸-tsiáu¹-**á**.
   (There are many sparrows in this tree.)

2. Lán¹ lé¹-**pài** tàu²-**tīn** lâi⁷-khì²⁻¹ peh²-**suann**. / Lé¹-**pài** lán¹ tàu²-**tīn** lâi⁷-khì²⁻¹ peh²-**suann**.
   (Let's go hiking together on Sunday.)

3. Guá¹ bē³-hiáu¹ tshiùnn² hit⁸ tiâu⁷ **kua**. / Hit⁸ tiâu⁷ **kua** guá¹ bē³-hiáu¹ **tshiùnn**.
   (I don't know how to sing that song.)

E04 Audio:

1. Guá¹ kah²⁻¹ i⁷ tī³ tshiū⁷-á¹-**kha** teh²⁻¹ tshiùnn²-**kua**. /
   Guá¹ kah²⁻¹ i⁷ teh²⁻¹ tshiū⁷-á¹-**kha** tshiùnn²-**kua**.
   I'm singing with her under the tree.

2. I⁷ kánn¹-ná¹ tsin⁷ siong⁷-**sim**. / I⁷ kánn¹-ná¹ tsiânn⁷ siong⁷-**sim**.
   He seems really sad.

SHORT TAKES

LESSON 12

Main Dialogue with Tone Markings

Tso̍h--ji̍t⁰ guán¹ tsa⁷-bóo¹-**kiánn** tsò²-senn⁷-**ji̍t**.

I⁷ siu⁷-tio̍h³ tsin⁷ tsē³ lé¹-**bu̍t**.

Koh²⁻¹ ū³ tsi̍t⁴ kha⁷ suān³-tsio̍h³ tshiú¹-**tsí**,

M̄³ tsai⁷ siánn¹-**lâng sàng**--ê⁰!

E01   h, d, b, j, g, f, c, i, a, e

E02
1. Guā³-**kháu** hit⁸ ê⁷ tsa⁷-poo⁷ gín¹-**á** sī³ (siánn¹-mih²⁻¹-**lâng**)?
   <u>Who</u> is that boy outside?

2. Guá¹ (**tso̍h**--ji̍t⁰) kah²⁻¹ in⁷ ang⁷-á¹-**bóo** tàu²-**tīn** khì²⁻¹ peh²-**suann**.
   I went mountain climbing with the couple <u>the day before yesterday</u>.

3. Lí¹ khuànn² tsit⁸ kha⁷ kim⁷-(**tshiú¹-tsí**) ū³ suí--bô⁰?
   What do you think? Is this golden <u>ring</u> beautiful?

4. Lín¹ tuā³-hàn² (tsa⁷-bóo¹-**kiánn**) tsiânn⁷ ài² tshiùnn²-**kua**.
   Your older <u>daughter</u> really likes singing.

5. Tse lāi³-**té** (m̄³ tsai⁷) sī³ siánn¹-**huè**?
   <u>I wonder</u> what's inside this.

6. Hit⁸ king⁷ kong⁷-**si** tsò² (suān³-**tsio̍h**) ê⁷ bé¹-**bē**.
   That company trades in <u>diamond</u>.

7. Lí¹ kià ê⁷ phue, guá¹ bô⁷ (siu--tio̍h⁰).
   I didn't <u>receive</u> the letter you sent me.

ANSWER KEY

8. I^7 sàng^2 lí^1 siánn^1-mih$^{2-1}$ sìng^2-tàn^2 (lé^1-**but**)?
   What Christmas <u>gift</u> did she give you?

E03 **Audio:**

1. Guán^1 hāu^3-**senn āu**--jit^0 tsò^2-senn^7-**jit**. / Guán^1 kiánn āu--jit^0 tsò^2-senn^7-**jit**.
   My son is celebrating his birthday the day after tomorrow.

2. Hit^8 tiâu^7 phuah^3-**liān** sī^3 gîn--ê^0. / Hit^8 ê^7 phuah^3-**liān** sī^3 gîn--ê^0.
   That necklace is (made of) silver.

3. Guá^1 m̄^{3} tsai^7-iánn^1 i^7 sī^3 siánn^1-mih$^{2-1}$ khuán^1 **lâng**.
   I don't know what kind of person he is.

LESSON 13

Main Dialogue with Tone Markings

Guá^1 thâu^7-tú^1-**á** teh$^{2-1}$ **kiò**--lí^0, lí^1 kám^1 bô^7 **thiann**--tio̍h^0?

Ū^3-**iánn**--ooh^0? Pháinn^1-**sè**--lah^0, guá^1 bô^7 tsù^2-**ì**.

Guá^1 tú^1-**tsiah** kòo^2 teh$^{2-1}$ sńg^1 tshiú^1-ki^7-**á**,

tú^1-hó^1 teh$^{2-1}$-beh$^{2-1}$ phò^2-**kuan**--ah^0!

E01   b, j, a, f, g, e, i, d, h, c

E02

1. Guá^1 (teh$^{2-1}$-beh$^{2-1}$) kàu^2-**uī**--ah^0!
   I am <u>almost</u> there!

2. Lí^1 kám^1 ū^3 (thiann^7-tio̍h^3) lán^1 ê^7 **kua**?
   Did you <u>hear</u> our song? / Do you <u>hear</u> the people sing?

3. (Thâu^7-tú^1-**á**) ū^3 tsit^4 tsiah^2 niau^7-**á** peh^2-khí^1-lí$^{2-1}$ tsit^8 tsâng^7 tshiū^7-á^1-**tíng**.
   A cat climbed up this tree <u>just a moment ago</u>.

4. A⁷-**kong** (kiò²) guá¹ khì²⁻¹ kám¹-á¹-**tiàm** bé¹ la̍k⁴ kuàn² **tsiú**.
   Grandpa <u>asked</u> me to buy six bottles of liquor at the grocery store.

5. In⁷ kui⁷-**kang** teh²⁻¹ (sńg¹ tshiú¹-ki⁷-**á**), m̄³ tsai¹ sī³ teh²⁻¹ sńg¹ **siánn**?
   They've been <u>fiddling with their phones</u> all day. Who knows what game they are playing.

6. I⁷ kóng¹-uē tsiok⁸ sè²-**siann**, lí¹ ài² (tsù²-ì²) thiann.
   He speaks very quietly, so you will have to listen <u>closely</u>.

E03
1. Tse Tâi⁷-gí kiò²-tsò² **siánn**?
   What is this called in Taiwanese? / How do you say this in Taiwanese?

2. Lí¹ ū³-iánn¹ khuànn²-tio̍h³ i⁷--ooh⁰?
   Oh, really? You saw him/her? / Wow, is it true that you saw him/her?!

3. Thiann⁷-kóng¹ i⁷ phò²-**sán**--ah⁰.
   I heard that that he/she went bankrupt.

4. Guá¹ siūnn³-beh²⁻¹ bé¹ tsi̍t⁴ tâi⁷ tiān³-**náu** hōo³ guán¹ tsa⁷-bóo¹-**kiánn**.
   I would like to buy a computer for my daughter. / I'm thinking about buying a computer for my daughter.

E04 Audio:

1. I⁷ kiò² guá¹ kòo² gín¹-**á**. / I⁷ kiò² guá¹ tsiàu²-kòo² gín¹-**á**.
   She told me to look after the kids.

2. Guá¹ tú¹-**tsiah** thiann⁷-tio̍h³ i⁷ teh²⁻¹ kiò² kíng¹-**tshat**! /
   Guá¹ tú¹-**á** thiann⁷-tio̍h³ i⁷ teh²⁻¹ kiò² kíng¹-**tshat**!
   I just heard him calling the police!

LESSON 14

Main Dialogue with Tone Markings

Ông--ê⁰ ta̍k⁴-ji̍t tshit⁸ tiám khí--lâi⁰,

liân⁷ tsá¹-tn̂g to⁷ bô⁷ tsia̍h, suî⁷ khì²⁻¹ phah² nâ⁷-kiû.

M̄³ tsai⁷ i⁷ sī³-án¹-tsuánn tsiah²⁻¹-nī³ ū³ khuì²-la̍t?

E01   f, j, d, a, i, e, b, h, c, g

E02

1. Táng--ê⁰ tsa⁷-hng (sī³-án¹-tsuánn) bô⁷ lâi?
   <u>Why</u> didn't our chairman come yesterday?

2. Ū--lah⁰. I⁷ lâi⁷ bô⁷ nn̄g³ hun⁷-tsing (suî⁷) tsáu--ah⁰.
   Yes, he did. He came for not more than two minutes and then left <u>right away</u>.

3. Guá¹ kin⁷-á¹-ji̍t bô⁷-îng⁷ kah²⁻¹ (liân⁷) tiong⁷-tàu (to⁷) bô⁷ tsia̍h.
   Today I was so busy that I didn't <u>even</u> have lunch.

4. Lán¹ bîn⁷-á¹-tsài (tsá¹-tn̂g) beh²⁻¹ tsia̍h³ siánn?
   What are we going to eat for <u>breakfast</u> tomorrow?

5. Lín¹ kiánn uī³-siánn¹-mih (tsiah²⁻¹-nī³) siong⁷-sim?
   Why is your son <u>so</u> sad?

6. In⁷ lâm⁷ pîng⁷-iú beh²⁻¹ khì²⁻¹ Ing⁷-kok (tshit⁸) kang.
   His boyfriend is going to England for <u>seven</u> days.

7. In⁷ e⁷-poo kah²⁻¹ Tân--ê⁰ khì²⁻¹ (phah² nâ⁷-kiû).
   They went to <u>play basketball</u> with Tan in the afternoon.

8. Guá¹ tú¹-á khì²⁻¹ ūn³-tōng, tsit⁸-má bô⁷ (khuì²-la̍t)--ah⁰.
   I just went to exercise. I don't have any <u>energy</u> now.

E03

1. Toh²-tíng (tsit⁸) ki⁷ tshiú¹-ki⁷-á sī³ siánn¹-lâng--ê⁰?
   Whose phone is <u>this</u> on the desk?

2. (Tsia ê⁷) sann sī³ beh²⁻¹ sàng--lâng⁰--ê⁰.
   <u>These</u> clothes are to be given away as gifts.

3. Tshiū⁷-á (hia) ū³ tsit⁴ liȧp⁴ tsiok⁸ tuā³ liȧp ê⁷ tsiȯh³-thâu.
   There is a large piece of stone <u>over there</u> by the tree.

4. Khuànn² i⁷ (hiah²⁻¹-nī³) huann⁷-hí, guá¹ mā³ tsin⁷ huann⁷-hí.
   Seeing that she is <u>so</u> happy, I'm also very happy.

E04 **Audio:**

1. Guá¹ liâm⁷-mi⁷ lâi. / Guá¹ suî⁷ lâi.
   I will come right away.

2. I⁷ tsin⁷ ū³-la̍t. / I⁷ tsiânn⁷ ū³-la̍t.
   She is really strong.

3. Ronaldo sī³ that⁸ kha⁷-kiû--ê⁰, m̄³ sī³ phah² the⁷-ní¹-suh--ê⁰!
   Ronaldo is a soccer player, not a tennis player!

LESSON 15

Main Dialogue with Tone Markings

Tsit⁸ siang⁷ âng⁷ phuê⁷-ê guá¹ kah²-ì sī³ kah²-ì,

m̄³-koh²⁻¹ bô⁷ ha̍h³ kha.

Pinn--á⁰ hit⁸ sann⁷ siang mā³ tsiânn⁷ suí,

m̄³-koh²⁻¹ lóng¹ siunn⁷ kuì.

E01   c, a, i, h, g, d, f, j, e, b

ANSWER KEY

E02

1. Lí¹ kóng¹-**uē** (siunn⁷) sè²-**siann**, guá¹ bô⁷ **thiann**--tio̍h⁰.
   You were speaking <u>too</u> quietly, so I didn't hear it.

2. Hit⁸ niá¹ **kûn** lí¹ ū³ (kah²-**ì**)--bô⁰?
   Did you <u>like</u> that skirt?

3. Guán¹ a⁷-**tsí** tī³ pah²-huè² kong⁷-**si** bé¹ tshit⁸ (siang⁷) bue̍h⁷-**á**.
   My big sister bought seven <u>pairs</u> of socks at the department store.

4. Lîm--ê⁰ tsiok⁸ ài² ūn³-**tōng**, ta̍k⁴-**kang** (lóng¹) khì²⁻¹ phah² nâ⁷-**kiû**.
   Lim loves sports. He goes to play basketball every day.

5. Guá¹ tiong⁷-**tàu** ū³ tsia̍h³ sī³ ū³ tsia̍h³, (m̄-koh²⁻¹) tsia̍h³ bô⁷ tsē.
   I did have lunch, <u>but</u> I didn't eat much.

6. Tsit⁸ ki⁷ tshiú¹-ki⁷-**á** sī³-án¹-**tsuánn** tsiah²⁻¹-nī³ (kuì)?
   Why is this cell phone so <u>expensive</u>?

7. Guán¹ tau tuà² tī³ iā³-**tshī** (pinn--á⁰).
   I live <u>beside</u> the night market. / My place is <u>next to</u> a night market.

E03

1. Tsit⁸ niá¹ **sann** bô⁷ ha̍h³-**su**.
   This piece of clothing doesn't fit.

2. Tsia--ê⁰ lóng¹-**tsóng** kuí¹ khoo⁷ **gîn**?
   How much are these in total?

3. I⁷ ê⁷ phuê⁷-**ê** sī³ lōo³-pinn⁷-tànn¹-**á bé**--ê⁰.
   His leather shoes were bought from a street vendor.

E04 Audio:

1. Hit⁸ siang⁷ ê guā³-tsē³ **tsînn**? / Hit⁸ siang⁷ ê kuí¹ khoo⁷ **gîn**?
   How much is that pair of shoes?

2. Âng⁷-**tsiú**, âng⁷-**tê** lóng¹ sī³ âng⁷-**sik**--ê⁰.
   Red wine, black tea, (they) are both red.

LESSON 16

Main Dialogue with Tone Markings

Tuì² **tsia** khiâ⁷ thih²-**bé** kàu² hué¹-tshia⁷-**thâu**,

phóo¹-thong⁷ **lâng** tio̍h³-ài² sī²-tsa̍p⁴-gōo³ **hun**.

Iah²⁻¹ nā³ **guá**, puànn² tiám¹-**tsing** bô⁷ kàu²-uī,

lí¹ tō³ hó¹ thang⁷ kiò² kíng¹-**tshat**--ah⁰!

E01 b, f, j, g, h, e, c, i, a, d

E02

1. Lí¹ kám¹ ē³-hiáu¹ (khiâ⁷) oo⁷-tóo¹-bái?
   Do you know how to <u>ride</u> a scooter?

2. Lí¹ khiâ⁷-**tshia** (tio̍h³-ài²) sè²-jī.
   Be careful when you ride.

3. Guán¹ **ang** tsin⁷ kah²-ì² hit⁸ tâi⁷ âng⁷ (thih²-**bé**).
   My husband really likes that red <u>bike</u>.

4. Guá¹ (phóo¹-**thong**) tshit⁸ tiám¹ **puànn** tsia̍h³ tsá¹-**tǹg**, tshit⁸ tiám¹ (sī²-tsa̍p⁴-gōo³) hun tshut⁸-**mn̂g**.
   I <u>usually</u> have my breakfast at half past seven, and go out at <u>a quarter to</u> eight.

5. (Tuì²) guán¹ tau kiânn⁷ khì²⁻¹ kong⁷ tshia⁷ pâi¹ á bô⁷ tsiok⁸ hn̄g, gōo³ hun⁷-tsing (tō³) kàu--ah⁰.
   It is not very far to walk <u>from</u> my place to the bus stop; you will get there in <u>just</u> five minutes.

6. Kin⁷-á¹-**jit** (hué¹-tshia⁷-**thâu**) tı̍k⁴-pia̍t⁴ lāu³-**jia̍t**.
   The <u>train station</u> is extraordinarily busy today.

E03

1. Nā³ siunn⁷ **kuì** tō³ m̄³-thang⁷ **bé**.
   (Don't buy it if it's too expensive.)

204   Answer Key

ANSWER KEY

2. Guá¹ tíng¹-pái tsáu¹ m̄³-tio̍h³ uī.
   (I went to the wrong place last time.)

E04 Audio:

1. Guá¹ sì² tiám¹ tsa̍p⁴-gōo³ hun ē³ kàu²-uī. / Guá¹ sì² tiám¹ tsa̍p⁴-gōo³ hun kàu.
   I will arrive at 4:15.

2. Guá¹ tuì² Hân⁷-kok lâi. / Guá¹ sī³ tuì² Hân⁷-kok lâi--ê⁰.
   I come from Korea.

LESSON 17

Main Dialogue with Tone Markings

Guá¹ puànn²-mê⁷-á pak⁸-**tóo-iau**,

khui⁷ ping⁷-**siunn** beh²⁻¹ tshuē³ mi̍h³-**kiānn tsia̍h**,

kan⁷-na⁷ tshuē³-tio̍h³ puànn² kuàn² í¹-king⁷ tshàu²-**sng** ê⁷ gû⁷-**ling**.

E01 g, i, a, f, d, b, j, e, c, h

E02

1. (Ping⁷-**siunn**) lāi³-té ū³ gōo³ lia̍p⁴ suāinn⁷-**á**.
   There are five mangoes in the <u>fridge</u>.

2. Ông--sian⁰-sinn⁰ (kan⁷-na⁷) pài²-la̍k tsiah²⁻¹ ū³-îng.
   Mr. Ong is available <u>only</u> on Saturdays.

3. Guá¹ kah²⁻¹ a⁷-**má** beh²⁻¹ khì²⁻¹ tshī³-tiûnn bé¹ (mi̍h³-**kiānn**).
   Grandma and I are going to the market to do some shopping.

4. Toh²-**tíng** hit⁸ pue⁷ si⁷-kue⁷-**tsiap** (tshàu²-**sng**)--ah⁰.
   That glass of watermelon juice on the table has <u>gone sour</u>.

SHORT TAKES

5. I⁷-**sing** kiò² lí¹ m̄³-thang⁷ iōng³ (gû⁷-**ling**) tshī³ niau⁷-á.
   The doctor told you not to feed cow's milk to the cat.

6. Tshù²-**lāi** ū³-kàu² jua̍h! Lí¹ khì²⁻¹ (khui⁷) thang⁷-á, hó--bô⁰?
   It's terribly hot in the house! Go open the windows, would you?

7. I⁷ thâu⁷-tú¹-á tsiah²⁻¹ tsia̍h³-pá, tsit⁸-**má** iū³-koh²⁻¹ (pak⁸-**tóo-iau**)--ah⁰!
   She was full just a while ago, and now she's hungry again!

8. Guá¹ ê⁷ tshiú¹-ki⁷-á m̄³ tsai⁷ tsáu¹ khì²⁻¹ tó¹-**uī**, sī²-kè lóng¹ (tshuē³) bô.
   I wonder where my cell phone has gone; I couldn't find it anywhere.

9. Lí¹ **sàng** ê⁷ lé¹-**bu̍t**, guá¹ (î¹-king⁷) siu--tio̍h⁰--ah⁰.
   I have already received the gift you sent me.

10. Tsuè²-**kīn** a⁷-kong tiānn³-tiānn³ (puànn²-mê⁷-á) tshut⁸-khì²⁻¹ sàn²-**pōo**.
    Lately, grandpa has frequently gone for a stroll in the middle of the night.

E03

1. Guá¹ tsin⁷ tshuì²-**ta**, tsia kám¹ ū³ **tsuí** thang⁷ lim?
   I'm really thirsty. Is there water to drink here?

2. Hit⁸ king⁷ **tiàm** sing⁷-lí tsiok⁸ **bái**, î¹-king⁷ kuainn⁷ **tiàm**--ah⁰.
   That shop's business was very bad, so it has already closed up shop.

E04 **Audio:**

1. Tse bí¹-**ling** tsin⁷ phang! / Bí¹-**ling** tsin⁷ phang!
   The rice milk smells really good!

2. Guá¹ beh²⁻¹ nn̄g³ pue⁷ ping⁷ tāu³-**ling**.
   I'd like two cups of iced soy milk.

LESSON 18

Main Dialogue with Tone Markings

Tshù²-lāi báng tsiok⁸ kāu,

Tit⁴-tit⁴ lâi⁷ kā³ guá¹ tshá, kā³ guá¹ tìng,

hāi³ guá¹ kui⁷-mê bē³ khùn--tit⁰,

siōng³-pan mā³ bô⁷ tsing⁷-sîn.

E01   a, g, h, d, b, f, c, j, i, e

E02

1. Tâi⁷-pak (tit⁴-tit⁴) lȯh³-hōo.
   It <u>keeps</u> raining in Taipei.

2. Guā³-kháu siunn⁷ (tshá), lán¹ lâi⁷-khì²⁻¹ lāi³-té kóng.
   It's too <u>noisy</u> outside; let's go inside to talk.

3. I⁷ ê⁷ kha khì²⁻¹ hōo³ (báng) tìng--tiȯh⁰.
   His leg got bitten by a <u>mosquito</u>.

4. Guá¹ ê⁷ tshiú¹-ki⁷-á hōo³ guán¹ pîng⁷-iú sńg¹ kah²⁻¹ (hāi)--khì⁰.
   My cell phone got <u>damaged</u> because my friend messed around with it.

5. Guán¹ sió¹-muē tiānn³-tiānn³ khiâ⁷ oo⁷-tóo¹-bái (siōng³-pan).
   My sister often <u>goes to work</u> by motorcycle.

6. Hit⁸ kuàn² gû⁷-ling tshàu²-sng--khì⁰, (bē³) lim (--tit⁰)--ah⁰!
   That bottle of milk has gone sour and has become/is now <u>undrinkable</u>.

7. Tân⁷ thài²-thài siū⁷-tiȯh³ hit⁸ tiunn⁷ phue, huân⁷-ló¹ kah²⁻¹ bē³ tsiȧh bē³ (khùn)--tit⁰.
   Having received that letter, Mrs. Tan got so worried that she couldn't eat or <u>sleep</u>.

8. Kin⁷-á¹-jit tsiânn⁷ kuânn, ài² tshīng³ tsit⁴ niá¹ (kāu) ê⁷ phòng²-se⁷-sann, tsiah²⁻¹ bē³ kuânn--tiȯh⁰.
   It's really cold today. You should wear a <u>heavy</u> sweater so you won't catch a cold.

E03

1. In⁷ hioh²-khùn²-ji̍t lóng¹ ē³ khì²⁻¹ that⁸ kha⁷-kiû. /
   Hioh²-khùn²-ji̍t in⁷ lóng¹ ē³ khì²⁻¹ that⁸ kha⁷-kiû.
   (Every holiday they would go play soccer.)

2. Nā³ bô⁷ siá--lo̍h⁰-lâi⁰, guá¹ liâm⁷-mi⁷ tō³ bē³-kì--tit⁰. /
   Guá¹ nā³ bô⁷ siá--lo̍h⁰-lâi⁰, liâm⁷-mi⁷ tō³ bē³-kì--tit⁰.
   (If I don't write it down, I will forget it right away.)

3. Guá¹ tsa⁷-mê bô⁷ khùn, tsái¹-khí siōng³-khò tsiok⁸ bô⁷ tsing⁷-sîn.
   (I didn't sleep last night, so I was so tired in class this morning.)

4. I⁷ tit⁴-tit⁴ tshá, hāi³ guá¹ bē³-kì²-tit⁸ beh²⁻¹ kóng¹ siánn.
   (She kept making noises, which made me forget what I wanted to say)

E04 **Audio:**

1. I⁷ tsing⁷-sîn--ah⁰. / I⁷ tshénn--ah⁰.
   He has woken up.

2. Pháinn¹-sè, guá¹ bē³-tàng² kā³ lí¹ kóng.
   Sorry, I can't tell you.

LESSON 19

Main Dialogue with Tone Markings

Piān³-sóo ê⁷ tiān³-hué pháinn--khì⁰,

Kui⁷ lāi³-té àm²-bîn⁷-bong.

I⁷ siūnn³-tio̍h³ tsa⁷-mê khuànn ê⁷ kuí¹-á¹-phìnn,

Kiann⁷ kah²⁻¹ m̄³ kánn¹ ji̍p⁴-khì²⁻¹ pàng²-jiō.

E01 h, b, a, i, j, d, g, c, f, e

ANSWER KEY

E02

1. I⁷ siūnn³-beh²⁻¹ (pàng²-jiō), suah² tshuē³-bô⁷ (piān³-sóo).
   He wants to <u>pee</u>, but he can't find a <u>toilet</u>.

2. Tshù²-lāi (àm²-bîn⁷-bong), guá¹ lâi⁷-khì²⁻¹ khui⁷ (tiān³-hué).
   <u>It's so dark</u> in the house; I'll go turn the <u>lights</u> on.

3. (Siūnn³-tioh³) āu³ kò² gueh beh²⁻¹ khì²⁻¹ Jit⁴-pún, guá¹ tō³ tsiok⁸ huann⁷-hí.
   Just <u>thinking that</u> I'm going to Japan next month already makes me so happy.

4. Tsiânn⁷ hāi! Guá¹ ê⁷ tiān³-náu kánn¹-ná¹ (pháinn--khì⁰)--ah⁰!
   Oh no! My computer seems <u>to be broken</u>!

5. I⁷ ê⁷ lú¹ pîng⁷-iú tsin⁷ ài² khuànn² tiān³-iánn, liân⁷ (kuí¹-á¹-phìnn) mā³ tsiok⁸ ài² khuànn.
   Her girlfriend really likes to watch movies—even <u>ghost movies</u> she really loves to watch..

6. Lín¹ sī³-án¹-tsuánn m̄³ (kánn¹) kah²⁻¹ i⁷ kóng¹-uē?
   Why are you afraid of talking to her?

7. I⁷ beh²⁻¹ (jip⁴-khì²⁻¹) pâng⁷-king hioh²-khùn--ah⁰.
   He's going <u>into</u> the room to rest.

8. Pâng⁷-king⁷-lāi ū³ ka⁷-tsuah, hāi³ i⁷ (kiann⁷) kah²⁻¹ khùn²-bē³-khì.
   There's a cockroach in the room, which makes him so <u>scared</u> that he can't fall asleep.

E03

1. Guá¹ siánn¹-mih lóng¹ m̄³ kiann!
   I'm not afraid of anything!

2. Pháinn¹-sè, tshiánn¹-mn̄g piān³-sóo tī³ tó¹-uī?
   Excuse me, can you tell me where the restroom is?

SHORT TAKES

E04 **Audio:**

1. I⁷ kiann⁷ **kuí.**
   He's afraid of ghosts.

2. Guá¹ ê⁷ lài²-**tah bô**--khì⁰--ah⁰.
   My lighter is gone.

3. Hit⁸ ê⁷ iánn¹-**phìnn** tsin⁷ khióng¹-**pòo**, guá¹ m̄³ kánn¹ **khuànn.**
   That video is really terrifying. I don't dare to watch it.

LESSON 20

Main Dialogue with Tone Markings

A⁷-**tsik** ta̍k⁴-**pái lâi** ê⁷ **sî,** lóng¹ ē³ the̍h³ tsit⁴ a̍h³

Suī³-sū³ tsio⁷-kóo¹-lè²-**toh lâi⁷ sàng**--guán⁰.

I⁷ kóng¹ tsit⁴-sì²-**lâng** hiah²⁻¹-nī³ kan⁷-**khóo,**

Sóo¹-í¹ tio̍h³-ài² tsia̍h³ tsit⁴-kuá¹ **tinn**--ê⁰.

E01   d, b, e, h, g, j, c, i, f, a

E02

1. Tsit⁸ lia̍p⁴ liú¹-**ting** tsiânn⁷ (**tinn**).
   This orange is really <u>sweet</u>.

2. (A⁷-**tsik**), lí¹ tang⁷-**sî** beh²⁻¹ koh²⁻¹ khì²⁻¹ Hô⁷-**lan?**
   <u>Uncle (father's younger brother)</u>, when are you going to Holland again?

3. Toh²-**tíng** hit⁸ (a̍h³) thn̂g⁷-**á** senn⁷ tsiok⁸ tsē³ káu¹-**hiā.**
   The <u>box</u> of candies on the table attracted so many ants.

ANSWER KEY

4. Guá¹ khǹg² tī³ kheh²-**thiann** ê⁷ kheh¹-**á**, siánn¹-**lâng** (theh)--khì⁰?
   Who <u>took</u> away the box I put in the living room?

5. Guá¹ siūnn³-kóng¹ lín¹ í¹-king⁷ **tsai**--**ah**⁰, (sóo¹-í¹) bô⁷ kā³ lín¹ **kóng**.
   I thought you already knew, <u>so</u> I didn't tell you.

6. Hā³-**pan** (ê⁷ **sî**), lán¹ lâi⁷-khì²⁻¹ tsiah³ suāinn⁷-á¹-**ping**!
   Let's go eat mango shaved ice after work!

7. In⁷ āu³-**pái** beh²⁻¹ tsò²-huê¹ khì²⁻¹ (Suī³-**sū**) peh² **suann**.
   They are going to go hiking together in <u>Switzerland</u> next time.

8. Tsit⁸ ê⁷ (tsio⁷-kóo¹-lè²-**toh**) sī³-án¹-**tsuánn** tsiah²⁻¹-nī³ khóo?
   Why is this <u>chocolate</u> so bitter?

9. Tsò² lāu³-**pē** lāu³-**bú**--ê⁰, (tsit⁴-sì²-**lâng**) huân⁷-ló¹ gín¹-**á**.
   Being a parent, you're going to worry about your children <u>all of your life</u>.

E03

1. Tsàu²-**kha** ū³ bí¹-**hún**, lí¹ kám¹ beh²⁻¹ **tsiah**--**tsit**⁰-**kuá**⁰?
   (There are rice noodles in the kitchen; do you want to eat some?)

2. Tsiah³-**pn̄g** ê⁷ sî⁷-**tsūn**, m̄³-thang⁷ sńg¹ tshiú¹-ki⁷-**á**.
   (Don't play on your phone while you are eating.)

E04 Audio:

1. Pháinn¹-**sè**, guá¹ bô⁷ sî⁷-**kan**.
   Sorry, I don't have time.

2. Tsit⁸-**má** kuí¹ **tiám**?
   What time is it now?

3. Guán¹ a⁷-**kū** tī³ Se⁷-pan⁷-**gâ** tshut⁸-**sì**.
   My mother's brother was born in Spain.

SHORT TAKES

INDEX

S = Southern Common Dialect
N = Northern Common Dialect

WORD	漢字	ENGLISH	LESSON	PAGE
--ah	矣	(particle indicating an action is completed or a change of situation)	10	95
--bô?	…無？	(question marker)	6	62
--ê	的	the one/person/thing that is…, (particle) (indicating sb/sth already mentioned with an emphasis on certain attribute of it)	12	111
--khì	去	(verbal complement) gone, away	19	167
--lah	啦	(particle often used to express slight disagreement, impatience or persuasion)	7	71
--ooh	喔	(particle indicating surprise or persuasion, sometimes requesting further confirmation of the statement made)	13	118
--tio̍h	著	(resultative complement indicating the action is performed successfully or has a result)	12	110
--tio̍h	著	(resultative complement indicating the action is performed successfully or has a result)	13	117
…sī… m̄-koh	…是… 毋過	…does/is indeed…, but it's just that (usu. used to concede a point made but still with some reservation)	15	133
a-hiann	阿兄	big brother, older brother (trad.)	7	71
a-kīm	阿妗	wife of mother's brother	20	175
a-kong	阿公	grandpa	4	47
a-kū	阿舅	mother's brother	20	175
a-ḿ	阿姆	wife of father's older brother (aunt)	20	175
a-má	阿媽	grandma	4	47

INDEX

WORD	漢字	ENGLISH	LESSON	PAGE
a-peh	阿伯	father's older brother (uncle)	20	175
a-tsí / a-tsé	阿姊	big sister, older sister (trad.)	7	71
a-tsik	阿叔	father's younger brother (uncle)	20	175
a-tsím	阿嬸	wife of father's younger brother (aunt)	20	175
a̍h / a̍p	盒	box (of)	20	175
a̍h-á / a̍p-á	盒仔	box	20	175
ài	愛	must, to need to; to like; to feel like; (noun) love, affection	10	94
ài-khùn	愛睏	sleepy	18	160
ak	沃	to water (plants); to drench	9	86
ak-hue	沃花	to water flowers, to water the garden	9	86
ak-tsuí	沃水	to water (plants), to irrigate	9	86
àm	暗	dark; late; night	19	168
àm-bîn-bong / àm-mi-moo	暗眠摸	to be pitch black, to be very dark	19	168
àm-sî	暗時	evening	1	26
án-tsuánn	按怎	how	14	127
ang	翁	husband	8	78
âng	紅	red; popular; to be at the height of one's career	15	133
ang-(á-)bóo	翁(仔)某	husband and wife, married couple	8	78
âng-pau	紅包	red envelope (a monetary gift put in a red envelope given on the eve of Lunar New Year or special occasions such as weddings)	15	133
âng-sik	紅色	red color	15	133
âng-tê	紅茶	black tea	15	133
âng-tsiú	紅酒	red wine	15	133
āu kò gue̍h (S) / āu kò ge̍h (N)	後個月	next month	2	33
āu lé-pài	後禮拜	next week	2	33

WORD	漢字	ENGLISH	LESSON	PAGE
āu--jit (S) / āu--lit (N)	後日	the day after tomorrow	2, 12	33, 109
āu-jit (S) / āu-lit (N)	後日	some day in the future	12	109
āu-pái	後擺	next time; in the future	10	95
bah	肉	pork, meat	5	55
bái	穤	ugly, bad, awful	7	70
báng(-á)	蠓(仔)	mosquito	18	158
bé (S) / bué (N)	買	to buy, to purchase	8	77
bē (S) / buē (N)	袂	can't; won't; to not be/get/feel + adj	3	39
bē (S) / buē (N)	賣	to sell	8	77
bé mih(-kiānn) (S) / bué mngh(-kiānn) (N)	買物(件)	to buy things, to shop; shopping	17	150
bē tsiah--tit (S) / buē tsiah--eh (N)	袂食得	to be inedible	18	160
bé-bē (S) / bué-buē (N)	買賣	buying and selling; business, trade	8	77
bē-hiáu (S) / buē-hiáng (N)	袂曉	can't (not knowing how to)	3	39
bē-īng--tit (S) / buē-īng--eh (N)	袂用得	to be unusable/unworkable; to be unsuitable	18	160
bē-kì--tit (S) / buē-kì--eh (N)	袂記得	to forget, to be unable to remember	18	160
bē-tàng / bē-tit-thang	袂當 / 袂得通	cannot, to be able to, to not get to do sth	18	160
bē-tit (S) / buē-tit (N)	袂得	to be unable/impossible to (usu. because the circumstances don't allow)	18	160
bē-tshài--ê (S) / buē-tshài--ê (N)	賣菜的	the person who sells vegetables; vegetable vendor	14	125
beh / bueh	欲	to want; to be going to	1	26
bī	味	taste, smell, flavor	20	177
bí-hún	米粉	rice noodles, rice vermicelli	5	55
Bí-kok	美國	United States	2	32
bí-ling / bí-ni	米奶	rice milk (a breakfast drink usually made with rice, peanuts and sesame)	17	151
bîn-á-tsài / miâ-á-tsài	明仔載	tomorrow	8	77

INDEX

WORD	漢字	ENGLISH	LESSON	PAGE
bió / bió-tsing	秒 / 秒鐘	second	10	94
bô	無	to not have, to not exist, without; not, no; otherwise..., if not so...	2, 6	32, 62
bô ài	無愛	to not want (to), to not feel like; to dislike	10	94
bô m̄-tio̍h	無毋著	that's right; you are absolutely right	16	141
bô pn̄g thang tsia̍h	無飯通食	to have no rice/food to eat	16	143
bô tsing-sîn	無精神	without energy, tired, bushed	18	161
bô--ah	無矣	to not have anymore, gone	10	95
bô--khì	無去	to be gone, to disappear	19	167
bô-iánn	無影	untrue, false; not really	13	118
bô-îng	無閒	to be busy (with); to have no time	6	61
bô-kàu	無夠	to be not enough, insufficient; not ... enough	10	93
bô-tánn	無膽	cowardly, gutless, wimpy	19	168
bóo	某	wife	8	78
bue̍h-á (S) / be̍h-á (N)	襪仔	socks	15	133
ê	个	(general measure word)	2	32
ē	會	can; will likely; to become/get/feel + adj	3	39
ê (S) / uê (N)	鞋	shoes	15	133
ê sî(-tsūn)	的時(陣)	when, at/during the time that, while	20	176
ē-hiáu	會曉	to know how to do (sth that must be learned), can	3	39
ē-īng--tit / ē-īng--eh	會用得	to be usable/doable; to be suitable	18	160
ē-kha	下跤	under, underneath, underside (noun/adv/prep)	11	103
e-poo	下晡	afternoon	1	26
ē-tàng / ē-tit-thang	會當 / 會得通	can, to be able to, to get to do sth	18	160
ē-tit	會得	to be able/possible to	18	160
gîn (S) / gûn (N)	銀	silver; money	12	110

WORD	漢字	ENGLISH	LESSON	PAGE
gín-á	囡仔	child; little boy or girl	12	109
gōo	五	five	16	142
gōo-gue̍h-tseh / gōo-ji̍t-tseh	五月節 / 五日節	The Dragon Boat Festival (The 5th day of the 5th month on the traditional calendar)	16	142
gû	牛	cow, cattle	17	151
gû-ling / gû-ni	牛奶	milk (from cows)	17	151
guá	我	I, me	1	25
guā	外	outside; over, slightly more than (number)	7	69
Guá (sī) tsa-hng kàu--ê.	我(是)昨昏到的。	I came yesterday; It was yesterday that I arrived.	12	111
guá ê	我的	my, mine	1	25
Guá gōo tiám tō khí--lâi.	我五點就起來。	I wake up as early as five o'clock.	16	143
Guá kah lí lâi-khì.	我佮你來去。	I'll come with you.	11	104
guā-kháu	外口	outside (noun/adv/prep)	7	69
Guā-kok-lâng	外國人	foreigner	3	40
guā-tsē / luā-tsuē	偌濟	how many, how much	2	33
Guā-tsē tsînn / luā-tsuē tsînn?	偌濟錢?	How much (money)?	15	135
guán (S) / gún (N)	阮	we (excluding listener), us, our; my	1, 5	25, 54
guán ê (S) / gún ê (N)	阮的	our (excluding listener), ours	5	54
guán tau (S) / gún tau (N)	阮兜	my place, my home	10	93
hā-khò	下課	to get out of class, to finish class	18	161
hā-pan	下班	to get off work/duty	18	161
ha̍h	合	to suit, to fit, to be in accordance with	15	134
ha̍h kha	合跤	to fit (one's feet)	15	134
ha̍h-su	合軀	to fit (one's body)	15	134
hāi	害	to harm; to cause/make sb to (do something against one's will); to be damaged/broken, to go bad or spoil	18	159

WORD	漢字	ENGLISH	LESSON	PAGE
Hāi--ah!	害矣！	Oh, shoot! We're in deep trouble; I'm screwed/done for	18	159
hāi--khì	害去	to go bad or spoil; to be broken	18	159
hāi--lâng	害人	to do harm to people, to be harmful	18	159
Hân-kok	韓國	Korea	2	32
hán-tit	罕得	seldom, rarely	3	40
hāu-senn (S) / hāu-sinn (N)	後生	son	12	109
heh-kiann / hennh-kiann	嚇驚	to scare	19	168
hia	遐	there	14	127
hia--ê	遐的	those; those ones there	14	127
hiah(-nī)	遐(爾)	so, such (like that)	14	127
hīnn-kau (S) / hī-kau (N)	耳鈎	earring	12	110
hio̍h-á	葉仔	leaf	11	102
hioh-khùn	歇睏	to rest, to take a rest	18	160
hioh-khùn-jit (S) / hioh-khùn-lit (N)	歇睏日	holiday	18	160
hip-siòng / hip-siōng	翕相	to take a picture	7	69
hip-siòng-ki / hip-siōng-ki / siòng-ki / siōng-ki	翕相機 / 相機	camera	7	70
hit	彼	that + noun	6	64
hit ê / he	彼个 / 彼	that (one), that thing	6	64
hit kang	彼工	that day	6	64
hng	遠	far	10	93
hng-hng	遠遠	rather far; from far away, from/at a distance	10	93
hó	好	good, fine	6, 9	63, 85
hō	號	number	4	48
hó (thang)	好(通)	it's about time to; had better	16	143
hó lim	好啉	delicious, tasty, to taste good (drinks)	6	63
hó--ah	好矣	done, finished, to be good now	10	95

WORD	漢字	ENGLISH	LESSON	PAGE
hó--bô?	好 無？	How about…? (Is it) okay? Sounds good? (new)	6	63
hó--m̌?	好 毋？	How about…? (Is it) okay? Sounds good? (trad.)	6	63
hó-khuànn	好看	good-looking, pretty; interesting (a good read)	6	63
Hô-lân / Hô-lan	荷蘭	Holland; the Netherlands	20	175
hó-thinn	好天	sunny (day), fair weather	9	85
hó tsiȧh	好食	tasty, delicious	5	55
hong	風	wind	9	85
hong tsin thàu	風真透	the wind is really strong; it's windy	9	85
hōo	予	to give; to (someone); to let, allow (sb do sth); to be verb(-ed)oun by	3	41
hōo	雨	rain	9	85
hōo-mua	雨幔	raincoat	9	86
hōo-sann / hōo-i	雨衫 / 雨衣	raincoat; rain jacket, rainwear	9	86
hōo-suànn	雨傘	umbrella	9	86
huan-á-hué (S) / huan-á-hé (N)	番仔火	match (for lighting fire)	19	167
huân-ló	煩惱	worried, to be anxious about	11	103
huān-tsiá	患者	patient	6	63
huann-hí	歡喜	happy, delighted, glad	11	103
Huat-kok-lâng	法國人	French (people)	3	40
hué (S) / hé (N)	火	fire	19	167
hué-tshia (S) / hé-tshia (N)	火車	train	2	33
hué-tshia-thâu (S) / hé-tshia-thâu (N)	火車頭	train station	16	141
hui-ki / hue-lîng-ki	飛機 / 飛行機	plane	2	33
hun / hun-tsing	分 / 分鐘	minute	10	94
hún-tsiáu	粉鳥	pigeon	11	102

INDEX

WORD	漢字	ENGLISH	LESSON	PAGE
i	伊	he/she, him/her	3	39
i ê	伊 的	his, her, hers	3	39
I tsáu tuì tshī-tiûnn khì.	伊 走 對 市場 去。	He runs to/towards the market.	16	141
í-king	已經	already	17	151
i-sing	醫生	doctor, physician, surgeon	6	63
iá-buē (S) / iá-bē (N)	猶未	not yet	17	151
iá-kiû	野球	baseball	14	126
iā-tshī(-á)	夜市(仔)	night market	5	54
iah / ah	抑	or; as for, by the way (usu. used to introduce a different topic)	16	142
iah nā	抑 若	as for; yet if it were	16	142
iah nā bô / nā bô	抑 若 無 / 若 無	otherwise; if not so	16	142
iah-bô / ah-bô	抑無	otherwise; if not so...	7	71
iah-sī / ah-sī / iah / ah	抑是 / 抑	or	7	71
iánn	影	shadow; to glimpse, to take a brief look	13	118
iánn-phìnn	影片	movie, video (clip)	19	168
iau	枵	hungry	17	149
iáu-koh / á-koh	猶閣	still	5	55
iáu-m̄-koh / ah-m̄-koh	猶毋過	but, yet, however	15	134
ik-king-á	浴間仔	bathroom, shower room	19	167
in	個	they, them; his/her	3	39
in (nn̄g ê) ang-á-bóo	個(兩个)翁仔某	(they) the couple	8	78
in ê	個 的	their, theirs	3	39
in-uī	因為	because	20	176
îng	閒	free, idle	6	61
Ing-bûn	英文	English (language; written language)	3	39
Ing-gí (S) / Ing-gú (N)	英語	English (language)	3	39
Ing-kok	英國	United Kingdom	2	32

WORD	漢字	ENGLISH	LESSON	PAGE
Ing-kok-lâng	英國人	British (people)	3	40
íng-pái	往擺	earlier times, once, sometime in the past	10	95
it-tit	一直	constantly; straight on	18	158
iū-koh	又閣	again (usu. recurring event or repeated behavior); and also	5	55
jī lâu (S) / lī lâu (N)	二樓	second floor	4	48
jîn-sing (S) / lîn-sing (N)	人生	life, human life	20	176
jip (S) / lip (N)	入	to put in, to go in; in	19	169
jip--khì (S) / lip--khì (N)	入去	to get in, to go in; in (directional complement)	19	169
jip--lâi (S) / lip--lâi (N)	入來	to come in; in (directional complement)	19	169
jit (S) / lit (N)	日	day; the sun	14	125
jit--sî (S) / lit--sî (N)	日時	daytime, during the day	17	149
Jit-gí / Jit-pún-uē / Lit-gí / Lit-pún-uē	日語 / 日本話	Japanese (language)	3	39
Jit-pún (S) / Lit-pún (N)	日本	Japan	2	33
juah (S) / luah (N)	熱	hot (weather)	1	25
juah-thinn (S) / luah-thinn (N)	熱天	summer	1	25
kā	共	for, on behalf of, to, at, from, (object marker in the disposal construction)	18	159
kā guá phah	共我拍	to hit me	18	159
kā guá tìng	共我叮	to sting me, to bite me	18	159
kā i bé	共伊買	to buy from him; to buy for him	18	159
kā lâng kóng	共人講	to tell people/others	18	159
kā mn̂g khui--khui	共門開開	to make the door open, to open the door	18	159
ka-kī / ka-tī	家己	oneself, one's own	8	79
ka-kī-lâng / ka-tī-lâng	家己人	people on one's own side, one of us	8	79
ka-tsuah	虼蚻	cockroach	18	158
kah	甲	to the point/extent that; until	9	86

INDEX

WORD	漢字	ENGLISH	LESSON	PAGE
kah	佮	with, and; to go together, to come with, to be added to, to attach	11	104
kah-ì	佮意	to find sth. agreeable, to like	15	133
kam	甘	sweet (aftertaste), umami	20	177
kám	敢	(question marker to form rhetorical and general questions)	13	118
Kám án-ne? / Kám án-ni?	敢 按呢？	Is that so?	13	118
kám ē	敢 會	Will it...? Is it...?	13	118
kám sī...?	敢是…？	Is it / are you... ? (question the idea)	3	40
kám ū	敢 有	Did it...? Has it...? Does it have...?	13	118
kám-á-tiàm	簸仔店	grocery store; small retail store that sells a variety of household items	8	77
kám-kóng	敢講	Is it possible that...; Can it be that...?	13	118
Kám-un-tsiat / Kám-un-tseh	感恩節	Thanksgiving	8	77
kan-khóo	艱苦	suffering, miserable	11	103
kan-na	干焦	only, merely, no more than	17	150
kang	工	day	6	64
kánn	敢	dare; bold	19	168
kánn-ná	敢若	to seem like, as if, likely	11	103
káu	狗	dog	1	26
kàu	到	to reach (place, time, quantity), to arrive at; up to	10	94
kāu	厚	thick, dense; strong, concentrated; numerous, abundant	18	158
káu-á	狗仔	dog, puppy	1	26
kàu-giȧh	夠額	to be sufficient (number, amount, degree); satisfactory	10	93
káu-hiā	狗蟻	ant	18	158
kāu-uē	厚話	talkative; gossipy	18	158

WORD	漢字	ENGLISH	LESSON	PAGE
kàu-uī	到位	to arrive	10	94
kè-thîng-tshia / kè-tîng-tshia	計程車	taxi	2	33
kha	跤	legs and feet, lower limb; under, underneath	11	103
kha-ta̍h-tshia	跤踏車	bicycle	16	141
kheh-á	篋仔	box, case (usu. small, drawer-like, with or without a lid)	20	175
kheh-thiann	客廳	living room	19	167
khì	去	to go	1	26
khì--ah	去矣	It's gone; gone (died); We're doomed!	19	167
khí--lì / khí--khì	起去	to go up; to go up north; up	11	104
khí--lâi	起來	to come up, to get up; up	11	104
khí-hong	起風	to get/become windy	9	85
khí-tshù	起厝	to build a house	4	47
khiâ	騎	to ride	16	141
khiâ-bé	騎馬	to ride a horse; horse riding	16	141
khiâ-tshia	騎車	to ride a bike/vehicle	16	141
khióng-pòo	恐怖	terrifying, scary, horrible	19	168
khǹg	囥	to put; to put aside	20	175
khǹg--lo̍h	囥落	to put down	20	175
khó-ài	可愛	lovable	4	48
khóo	苦	bitter; tough	20	177
khuànn	看	to see; to watch, to look at; to read	6, 13	62, 117
khuànn tiān-iánn	看電影	to watch a movie	6	62
khuànn tsheh / khuànn tsu	看冊 / 看書	to read a book	6	62
khuànn--kìnn / khuàinn	看見	to see, to catch sight of	6	62
khuànn--tio̍h	看著	to see	13	117

INDEX

WORD	漢字	ENGLISH	LESSON	PAGE
khui	開	to open; to turn on; to start off, to set out; to issue (bills, checks, traffic tickets), to prescribe (medicine)	17	**150**
khui tiān-sī	開 電視	to turn on the TV	17	**150**
khuì-la̍t	氣力	strength, energy	14	**127**
khui-mn̂g	開門	to open the door	17	**150**
khùn	睏	to sleep	18	**160**
khùn--khì	睏去	to fall asleep	18	**160**
khùn-tàu	睏晝	to take a nap after lunch	18	**160**
kî-kuài	奇怪	strange, weird, unusual	16	**142**
kià	寄	to send, to mail; to entrust; to deposit	12	**110**
kiann	驚	scared, afraid (of); to scare	19	**168**
kiánn	囝	son; child (of a person); (diminutive suffix indicating small or a little)	12	**109**
kiânn	行	to walk; to move (chess, train, ship); to run (machinery, devices, vehicles)	10	**93**
kiann-á / kiann-eh	驚了 / 驚見	to be afraid that, to fear that	19	**168**
kiânn-lōo	行路	to walk, to go on foot	10	**93**
kim	金	gold, golden; money	12	**110**
kīn (S) / kūn (N)	近	close, near	10	**93**
kin-á-ji̍t (S) / kin-á-li̍t (N)	今仔日	today	1	**25**
kīn-lâi (S) / kūn-lâi (N)	近來	lately, recently	6	**63**
kin-tsio (S) / king-tsio (N)	弓蕉	banana	5	**56**
kiò	叫	to call; to summon; to tell/ask sb to do sth; to order (food)	13	**117**
kiò i lâi	叫 伊 來	to tell him/her to come	13	**117**
kiò kíng-tshat / kiò kìng-tshat	叫 警察	to call the police	13	**117**
kiò tsi̍t uánn mī	叫 一 碗 麵	to order a bowl of noodle	13	**117**

WORD	漢字	ENGLISH	LESSON	PAGE
kiò-tsò (S) / kiò-tsuè (N)	叫做	to be called	13	117
kiōng-beh	強欲	almost, nearly + verb (usu. against one's will)	13	119
kiû	球	ball	14	126
kng	光	bright, shiny; light	19	168
Ko-hiông-tshī	高雄市	Kaohsiung City	4	47
ko-ko / ko--ko	哥哥 / 哥哥	big brother, older brother (new)	7	71
koh	閣	and also, moreover; yet still; again; (not...) anymore	5	55
koh-tsài	閣再	once more, once again, over again	5	55
kok	國	country	2	32
kóng	講	to speak (language); to tell (story, joke, lie)	3	39
kóng tiān-uē	講電話	to talk on the phone	3	39
kong-si	公司	company	8	77
kong-tshia / bah-suh	公車 / (バス)	bus	2	33
kong-tshia-pâi-á / tshia-pâi-á	公車牌仔 / 車牌仔	bus stop (lit: the board for bus routes and timetables)	16	141
kóng-uē	講話	to talk, to speak	3	39
kòo	顧	to take care of; to be engrossed in sth, to be obsessed with sth	13	118
kòo gín-á	顧囡仔	to look after the children	13	118
kòo sńg	顧耍	to care only about playing (without thinking about anything else)	13	118
koo-niû	姑娘	girl, lady (trad., unmarried); miss; nun/Sister	7	69
kóo-tsui	古錐	cute, adorable (child, pet)	4	48
kua	歌	song	11	102
kuai	乖	tame, obedient, well-behaved (child, animal)	4	48
kuainn (S) / kuinn (N)	關	to close, to shut; to turn off	17	150

INDEX

WORD	漢字	ENGLISH	LESSON	PAGE
kuainn thang-á (S) / kuinn thang-á (N)	關窗仔	to close the window	17	150
kuainn tiàm (S) / kuinn tiàm (N)	關店	to close the store; to close up shop, to go out of business	17	150
kuan	關	checkpoint, pass; barrier, difficulty	13	119
kuàn	罐	can, jar, bottle (of)	5	56
kuânn	寒	cold (weather)	1	25
kuânn-thinn	寒天	winter	1	25
kué-tsí-tsiap / kó-tsiap	果子汁 / 果汁	fruit juice	5	56
kuí	鬼	ghost, spirit	19	168
kuí	幾	several, a couple of	20	176
kuì	貴	expensive; valued; honored (+ title/company)	15	135
Kuí ê?	幾个?	How many? (usu. countable and small number)	20	176
Kuí khoo gîn? (S) / Kuí khoo gûn? (N)	幾箍銀?	How much? (lit. how many dollars?)	15	135
kuí tiám	幾點	what time (o'clock)	20	176
kuí-á-phìnn	鬼仔片	ghost flick, ghost movie	19	168
kui-ê	規个	the whole, entire	9	87
kui-kang	規工	the whole day, all day	9	87
kui-mê (S) / kui-mî (N)	規暝	whole night	17	149
kui-sin-khu / kui-sing-khu	規身軀	the whole body; from head to toe	9	87
kuì-som-som / kuì-sam-sam	貴參參	to be very expensive	15	135
lâi	來	to come (to)	1, 5	26, 54
Lâi tsit uánn mī.	來一碗麵。	Bring me/I'll have a bowl of noodles. ("Lâi" can be used to order at a food stand or restaurant)	5	54
lâi-khì / lǎi	來去	to be/get going (usu. I or we); to leave	5	54
lài-tah	（ライター）	lighter	19	167

SHORT TAKES

WORD	漢字	ENGLISH	LESSON	PAGE
lāi-té (S) / lāi-tué (N)	內底	inside (noun/adv/prep)	7	69
la̍k	六	six	4	48
lâm pîng-iú	男朋友	boyfriend	3	40
lán	咱	we (including listener), us, our; you and me; let's	5	54
lán ê	咱的	our (including listener), ours	5	54
Lán lâi-khì + verb	咱來去…	Let's (go) + verb(-ing)	5	54
lâng	人	person, people; human	3	40
lâng bô sóng-khuài / bô sóng-khuài	人無爽快 / 無爽快	feeling unwell, sick	6	63
lâu	樓	floor; multi-story building	4	48
lāu-bú	老母	mother (trad.)	7	71
lāu-jia̍t (S) / lāu-lia̍t (N)	鬧熱	bustling, busy, crowded, lively	5	54
lāu-jia̍t kún-kún (S) / lāu-lia̍t kún-kún (N)	鬧熱滾滾	to be super busy and crowded; to bustle with noise and excitement	5	54
lâu-kha	樓跤	downstairs	4	48
lāu-pē	老爸	father (trad.)	7	71
lâu-tíng	樓頂	upstairs	4	48
lé	禮	gift, present; rite, etiquette, courtesy	12	110
lé-bu̍t	禮物	gift, present	12	110
lé-pài	禮拜	week; Sunday; church service	2, 6	33, 61
lé-pài-jit (S) / lé-pài lit (N)	禮拜日	Sunday	6	61
lí	你	you (singular)	1	25
Lí (nā) thiàu, guá tō thiàu.	你（若）跳，我就跳。	(If) you jump, I jump.	16	142
lí ê	你的	your (singular), yours	1	25
lí kah guá	你佮我	you and me	11	104
Lí tuì tó-(uī) lâi?	你對佗(位)來？	Where do/did you come from?	16	141

WORD	漢字	ENGLISH	LESSON	PAGE
liâm-mi	連鞭	immediately, right away	14	126
liân	連	to connect; in succession; even also	14	126
Liân i to tsai.	連 伊 都 知。	Even he knows.	14	126
liân...to / liâm...to	連...都	even	14	126
lim	啉	to drink	5	56
lim tê	啉 茶	to drink tea	5	56
lim thng	啉 湯	to eat/drink soup	5	56
lim tsuí	啉 水	to drink water	5	56
lim-tsiú-tsuì	啉酒醉	to be drunk	5	56
lín	恁	you (plural); your	1	26
lín ê	恁 的	your (plural), yours	1	26
lín tau	恁 兜	your place, your home	10	93
liú-ting-tsiap	柳丁汁	orange juice	5	56
lóh	落	to fall, to go down	9	85
lóh--khì / lueh	落去	to go down; to go down south; down	11	104
lóh--lâi / luaih	落來	to come down; down	11	104
lóh-hōo	落雨	to rain	9	86
lóh-hōo-thinn / hōo-lâi-thinn	落雨天 / 雨來天	rainy day	9	85
lóh-tshia	落車	to get off the bus/train, to get out of a car/taxi	9	85
lóng	攏	all (of), both, together	15	134
lóng-tsóng	攏總	(in) total, altogether; all	15	134
lóo-bah-pn̄g	滷肉飯	braised pork rice	5	55
lōo-pinn	路邊	roadside	15	134
lōo-pinn-tànn-á	路邊擔仔	street vendor, roadside stall	15	134
lú pîng-iú	女 朋友	girlfriend	3	40
m̄ kánn	毋 敢	dare not, to not have the courage/guts	19	168
m̄ sī	毋 是	to not be, isn't, aren't; no, wrong	3	40

WORD	漢字	ENGLISH	LESSON	PAGE
m̄ tsai	毋知	to not know; I wonder	12	110
m̄-koh	毋過	but	15	133
m̄-nā	毋但	not only	17	150
m̄-thang	毋通	don't, had better not to	16	143
m̄-tio̍h	毋著	wrong; to be incorrect	16	141
m̄-tsiah	毋才	that's why; only then, so that	10	94
mā	嘛	also, too	1	26
ma-ma / ma--ma	媽媽 / 媽媽	mother (new)	7	71
mê--sî (S) / mî--sî (N)	暝時	nighttime, during the night	17	149
me-me / me--me	妹妹 / 妹妹	little sister, younger sister (new)	7	71
mī	麵	noodles	2	34
mi̍h(-kiānn) (S) / mn̍gh(-kiānn) (N)	物(件)	(material) things; object, item	17	150
mn̂g	門	door	9	86
nā	若	if	16	142
niá	領	(measure word for clothes like shirts, pants, skirts, etc); neck, collar	8	78
niau	貓	cat	4	48
niau-á	貓仔	cat, kitty	4	48
nn̄g	兩	two	2	32
nn̄g (tsàn) lâu	兩(層)樓	two floors ("tsàn" is the measure word for floors, levels and steps of stairs)	4	48
nn̄g tsiah káu-á	兩隻狗仔	two dogs	2	32
Ông--ê	王的	Ong (Ong is a common Taiwanese family name; "--ê": suffix for addressing or referring to a person, often indicating familiarity)	14	125
ông-lâi-tsiap	王梨汁	pineapple juice	5	56
oo-tóo-bái / ki-tshia	(オートバイ) / 機車	motorcycle, scooter	16	141

INDEX

WORD	漢字	ENGLISH	LESSON	PAGE
pá	飽	full	17	149
pa-pa / pa--pa	爸爸 / 爸爸	father (new)	7	71
pah-huè kong-si (S) / pah-hè kong-si (N)	百貨 公司	department store	8	77
pài-gōo	拜五	Friday	6	61
pài-it	拜一	Monday	6	61
pài-jī (S) / pài-lī (N)	拜二	Tuesday	6	61
pài-la̍k	拜六	Saturday	6	61
pài-sann	拜三	Wednesday	6	61
pài-sì	拜四	Thursday	6	61
pak-tóo	腹肚	belly, stomach	17	149
pak-tóo-iau	腹肚枵	to be hungry	17	149
pàng-jiō (S) / pàng-liō (N)	放尿	to pee, to urinate	19	169
pâng-king	房間	room (in a house)	19	167
pàng-sái	放屎	to poop, to defecate	19	169
pa̍t-lâng	別人	another person, other people	8	79
peh	跖	to climb, to ascend	11	103
peh lâu-thui	跖 樓梯	to go up the stairs	11	104
peh--khí-khì / peh--khí-lì	跖 起去	to climb up (away from the speaker)	11	104
peh-suann	跖山	to climb a mountain; mountain hiking	11	103
pēnn-īnn (S) / pīnn-īnn (N)	病院	hospital	6	64
pēnn-lâng (S) / pīnn-lâng (N)	病人	patient	6	64
phah	拍	to hit, to beat; to attack, to fight; to cause (+ result); to play	14	126
phah nâ-kiû	拍 籃球	to play basketball	14	126
pháinn	歹	bad, evil, wicked	6, 9	63, 85
pháinn--khì	歹去	to be broken, out of order; to go bad, rotten	19	167
pháinn-sè	歹勢	excuse me, sorry; to feel embarrassed/shy	6	63

SHORT TAKES

WORD	漢字	ENGLISH	LESSON	PAGE
Pháinn-sè, guá beh lái piān-sóo--tsit-ē.	歹勢，我 欲 來去 便所 一下。	Excuse me, I need to use the restroom. I'll be right back.	19	169
pháinn-thinn	歹天	rainy (day), bad weather	9	85
phang	芳	fragrant, aromatic, sweet-smelling, delicious-smelling	17	151
phang	蜂	bee, wasp	18	158
phàu	泡	to infuse in hot water; to make (tea, hot chocolate, coffee, milk, etc)	2	34
phàu-mī	泡麵	instant ramen	2	34
phàu-tê	泡茶	to brew tea	2	34
phín-phóng / toh-kiû	（ピンポン）/ 桌球	table tennis, ping-pong	14	126
phò-kuan	破關	to beat the level/game	13	119
phò-sán	破產	to go broke, to be bankrupt	13	119
phông-kó / lìn-gooh	蘋果 / (りんご)	apple	5	56
phòng-se	膨紗	yarn	8	78
phòng-se-sann	膨紗衫	sweater, knitted garment	8	78
phóo-thong	普通	ordinary, normal; usually, normally	16	142
phuà--khì	破去	to be broken, to be worn-out/ripped	19	167
phuà-pēnn (S) / phuà-pīnn (N)	破病	to get sick, to fall ill	6	63
phua̍h-liān	袚鍊	necklace	12	110
phue	批	letter	3	41
phuê (S) / phë (N)	皮	skin, leather	15	133
phuê-ê (S) / phê-uê (N)	皮鞋	leather shoes	15	133
piān-sóo	便所	restroom, toilet	19	167
piánn	餅	cookie, cracker, cake (generic term for round flat pastries)	20	176
ping	冰	ice; ice-cold	17	150
pîng-iú	朋友	friend	2	32

INDEX

WORD	漢字	ENGLISH	LESSON	PAGE
ping-siunn	冰箱	fridge, freezer	17	150
pinn--á	邊仔	beside, next to; nearby; side	15	134
pn̄g	飯	rice (cooked)	5	55
po̍h	薄	thin; weak, watery	18	158
puànn	半	half, semi-, mid-; in the middle of	17	149
puànn tiám-tsing	半點鐘	half an hour	10	94
puànn tiám-tsing kú	半點鐘久	for half an hour	10	94
puànn-mê(-á) (S) / puànn-mî(-á) (N)	半暝(仔)	in the middle of the night, midnight	17	149
puann-tshù	搬厝	to move (house); house moving	4	48
pua̍t-á / pa̍t-á	菝仔	guava	5	56
pue	杯	cup (of), glass (of)	5	56
pue (S) / pe (N)	飛	to fly	11	102
pue--lo̍h-lâi (S) / pe--lo̍h-lâi (N)	飛落來	to fly down (towards the speaker)	11	104
pue-á	杯仔	cup, glass	5	56
sàn-pōo	散步	to go for a walk, to take a stroll	10	93
sàng	送	to give (as a present); to send, to deliver; to see sb off	8	78
sàng-lé	送禮	to give a present	8	78
sann	三	three	4	48
sann pue tsiú	三杯酒	three glasses of liquor/alcoholic drink	5	56
sann-(á-)khòo	衫(仔)褲	shirts and pants, clothes (in general)	8	78
sann-tǹg	三頓	three meals	4	48
sè (S) / suè (N)	細	small	8	79
sè-hàn (S) / suè-hàn (N)	細漢	short and small (body); the younger (birth order); in childhood	8	79
sè-jī (S) / suè-lī (N)	細膩	careful, cautious	13	118
Se-pan-gâ	西班牙	Spain	20	175
sè-siann (S) / suè-siann (N)	細聲	in a low/soft voice	8	79

WORD	漢字	ENGLISH	LESSON	PAGE
seh iâ-tshī	踅 夜市	to go for a stroll in a night market	5	54
senn (S) / sinn (N)	生	to give birth, to be born; to breed, to produce, to grow	12	109
senn-jit (S) / sinn-lit (N)	生日	birthday	12	109
sì	四	four	16	142
sī	是	to be; yes, right, correct	3	40
sī + ... + --ê / ... + --ê	是...的 / ...的	It was ... that, (particle used to emphasize a specific detail such as time, manner, person or place of an action or event.)	12	111
Sī i sàng--ê.	是 伊 送 的。	It was given by him; It was him who gave it to me.	12	111
sī-án-tsuánn	是按怎	why, how come (trad.)	14	127
sî-kan	時間	time, hours (for doing something); clock time	20	176
sì-kè (S) / sì-kuè (N)	四界	everywhere, anywhere	16	142
si-kue-tsiap	西瓜汁	watermelon juice	5	56
sī-m̄-sī...?	是毋是...?	Is it / are you...? (yes or no)	3	40
sì-tsap-gōo	四十五	forty-five	16	142
siá	寫	to write	3	41
siá phue	寫批	to write a letter	3	41
sian-sinn / sin-senn	先生	gentleman, sir; Mr.; teacher, doctor	7	69
siang	雙	a pair (of); two, even (number)	15	133
siang-tshiú	雙手	both hands, two hands	15	133
siánn-huè (S) / siánn-hè (N)	啥貨	what	12	111
siánn(-mih)	啥(物)	what; what + noun	12	111
siánn(-mih)-khuán	啥(物)款	what kind of; how	12	111
siánn(-mih)-lâng / siáng	啥(物)人	who	12	111
siàu-liân-lâng	少年人	young man	7	69

INDEX

WORD	漢字	ENGLISH	LESSON	PAGE
sim-lāi	心內	in one's heart/mind, inwardly	7	69
sîn	神	god, spirit	19	168
sin-khu / sing-khu	身軀	body	9	87
sin-pinn	身邊	at/by one's side; around oneself	15	134
sing-lí	生理	business, trade	8	77
sing-lí-lâng	生理人	businessperson	8	77
Sìng-tàn / Sìng-tàn-tsiat / Sìng-tàn-tseh	聖誕 / 聖誕節	Christmas	8	77
sió-khuá-á	小可仔	a little, a bit; slightly; a small amount of	15, 20	134, 176
sió-muē (S) / sió-bē (N)	小妹	little sister, younger sister (trad.)	7	70
sió-tī	小弟	little brother, younger brother (trad.)	7	70
sió-tsiá	小姐	lady; Ms	7	69
siȯk	俗	cheap	15	135
Siȯk sī siȯk, m̄-koh bô suí.	俗是俗，毋過無媠。	It is cheap, but just not very pretty.	15	134
siōng	像	portrait, picture, photograph	7	70
siōng-khò	上課	to go to class; at school	18	161
siōng-pan	上班	to go to work; at work	18	161
siòng-phìnn	相片	photo, picture	7	69
siong-sim	傷心	sad, grieved, heart-broken	11	103
sit-lé	失禮	sorry, my apologies	6	63
siu	收	to gather, to collect; to put away	12	110
siû	泅	to swim	1	26
siu--tiȯh	收著	to receive, to have received	12	110
siû-tsuí	泅水	to swim; swimming	1	26
siunn	傷	too, overly	15	134
siūnn	想	to think	19	168
siunn tāng	傷重	too heavy	15	134
siūnn--tiȯh	想著	to think of, to call to mind	19	168

WORD	漢字	ENGLISH	LESSON	PAGE
siunn-á	箱仔	large box, chest, case	17, 20	150, 175
siūnn-beh (S) / siūnn-bueh (N)	想欲	would like to; to want	1	26
siūnn-kóng	想講	to think that, to consider that	19	168
sng	酸	sour, acidic; aching	17	151
sńg	耍	to play, to toy with; to have fun, to mess around	13	119
sńg tiān-náu	耍 電腦	to play computer games	13	119
sńg tshiú-ki-á	耍 手機仔	to use a phone non-verbally (texting, reading, playing games, etc.); to be preoccupied with one's phone	13	119
sóng	爽	pleasant, feeling good, cheerful, joyful (informal)	6	63
sóng-khuài	爽快	pleasant, comfortable, refreshing	6	63
sóo-í	所以	therefore, so	20	176
sòo-jī (S) / sòo-lī (N)	數字	number, figure, numeral	4	48
suah	煞	(to end up...) unexpectedly; contrarily, instead, however (placed after the subj.)	9	85
suāinn-á	檨仔	mango	5	56
suān-tsio̍h	璇石	diamond	12	110
suí	媠	pretty, beautiful	7	70
suî	隨	to follow; right afterwards, straight away; each (...its own)	14	126
suí koo-niû	媠 姑娘	pretty girl	7	70
suí tsa-bóo	媠 查某	pretty woman	7	70
Suī-sū	瑞士	Switzerland	20	175
suí-tang-tang	媠噹噹	very beautiful, very pretty (usu. female after getting dressed up or made up)	7	70
Suī-tián	瑞典	Sweden	20	175
ta	焦	dry	9	86

INDEX

WORD	漢字	ENGLISH	LESSON	PAGE
Tâi-gí (S) / Tâi-gú (N)	台語	Taiwanese (language)	3	39
Tâi-lâm-tshī	台南市	Tainan City	4	47
Tâi-pak-tshī	台北市	Taipei City	4	47
Tâi-tiong-tshī	台中市	Taichung City	4	47
Tâi-uân	台灣	Taiwan	2	33
Tâi-uân-lâng	台灣人	Taiwanese (people)	3	40
Tâi-uân-uē	台灣話	Taiwanese (language)	3	39
ta̍k ê	逐个	everyone; each one (of them)	14	125
ta̍k-jit (S) / ta̍k-lit (N)	逐日	everyday	14	125
ta̍k-kang	逐工	everyday	14	125
ta̍k-ke	逐家	everyone, everybody	14	125
ta̍k-pái	逐擺	every time	14	125
tâm	澹	wet	9	86
tâm-lok-lok	澹漉漉	to be dripping wet	9	86
Tân--ê	陳的	Tan ("family name + --ê" usually refers to a man)	14	125
táng--ê	董的	chairman, director	14	125
tang-sî / tī-sî	當時 / 底時	when (in a question)	20	176
tau	兜	one's place, one's home (usu. used with a possessive pronoun)	10	93
tāu-ling / tāu-ni	豆奶	soy milk	17	151
tàu-tīn	鬥陣	together, jointly; to get along, to be together	11	104
teh-beh / tih-beh	咧欲	to be about to	13	119
thài-thài	太太	madam; Mrs.; wife	7	69
thang	通	may, can; (in order) to, so as to	16	143
thâng	蟲	worm; insect	18	158
that kha-kiû	踢 跤球	to play soccer	14	126
thàu-hong	透風	to start blowing strong wind, to pick up	9	85

WORD	漢字	ENGLISH	LESSON	PAGE
thâu-tú-á	頭拄仔	just now, just a moment ago	13	117
the-ní-suh / bāng-kiû	(テニス) / 網球	tennis	14	126
théh	提	to take, to get, to hold	20	175
thiám	忝	tired, exhausted; severe, thorough	18	161
thiann	聽	to listen to	13	117
thiann--tio̍h	聽著	to hear	13	117
thiann-kóng	聽講	to hear of; it's said that...	13	117
thih-bé	鐵馬	bicycle	16	141
thinn-khì	天氣	weather	9	85
thinn-tíng	天頂	in the sky; in heaven	11	103
thng	湯	soup	5	55
thǹg	褪	to take off (clothes); to fall out (baby teeth), to shed (skin)	8	79
thn̂g	糖	sugar	20	176
thn̂g-á	糖仔	candy	20	176
thn̂g-á-piánn	糖仔餅	candies and cookies, sweets	20	176
thó-ià	討厭	to find sth. disagreeable, to dislike	15	133
tī	佇	at/in; to be at/in	4	47
tī-leh / leh / teh	佇咧 / 咧 / 咧	to be verb(-ing) / to be present at (location)	4	47
ti-ti / ti--ti	弟弟 / 弟弟	little brother, younger brother (new)	7	70
tiàm	店	shop, store	8	77
tiām	恬	quiet, silent	18	158
tiām-tiām	恬恬	Be quiet! (as an order); quietly, silently	18	158
tiám-tsing	點鐘	hour	10	94
tiān	電	electricity, electric	19	167
tiān-hué (S) / tiān-hé (N)	電火	electric light, lamp	19	167
tiān-sī	電視	TV	6	62
tiān-tōng	電動	electric-powered; game console; video game	13	119

INDEX

WORD	漢字	ENGLISH	LESSON	PAGE
tiān-tsú phue	電子 批	email	3	41
tiān-uē	電話	telephone; phone call	13	119
tiānn-tiānn	定定	often, frequently	3	40
tik-(á-)nâ	竹(仔)林	bamboo grove, bamboo forest	11	102
tik-piàt	特別	special; specially, extraordinarily	16	142
tíng	頂	on, on the top of, above; (measure word for hats)	11	103
tìng	叮	to sting (insect)	18	159
tíng-kuân	頂懸	on, above, upside (noun /adv/prep)	11	103
tíng-pái	頂擺	last time	10	95
tinn	甜	sweet, sugary	20	177
tio̍h	著	Yes, right; to be correct, to hit the mark; to achieve; to catch (a disease); should, need to, ought to	16	141
tio̍h-ài	著愛	should, need to, ought to	16	141
tit	直	straight, upright; direct, blunt	18	158
tit-tit	直直	constantly; directly; squarely; straight on	18	158
tǹg	頓	meal	14	127
to	都	(adv. used in a clause with the idea of indeed, yet, still, even, all)	14	126
tō / tiō	就	then; just	16	142
tō sī / tiō sī	就是	just, exactly; to be exactly sb/sth	16	143
tó-uī / toh	佗位 / 佗	where	10	94
toh-tíng	桌頂	on the table; on the desk	11	103
too-tshī	都市	(big) city	4	47
tsa-bóo gín-á	查某 囡仔	girl	12	109
tsa-bóo pîng-iú	查某 朋友	girlfriend; female friend	3	40
tsa-bóo-kiánn / tsa̋u-kiánn	查某囝	daughter	12	109

SHORT TAKES 237

WORD	漢字	ENGLISH	LESSON	PAGE
tsa-hng / tsǎng	昨昏	yesterday	8	77
tsa-mê (S) / tsa-mî (N)	昨暝	last night	17	149
tsa-poo gín-á	查埔 囡仔	boy	12	109
tsa-poo pîng-iú	查埔 朋友	boyfriend; male friend	3	40
tsá-tǹg / tsái-khí-tǹg	早頓 / 早起頓	breakfast	14	127
tsah	紮	to bring, to carry with one (usu. smaller items in one's pocket or bag)	2	33
tsah piān-tong	紮 便當	to carry a lunchbox ("bento")	2	33
tsah tsînn	紮 錢	to bring/have money in one's pocket	2	33
tsái-khí / tsá-khí	早起	morning	1	26
tsai(-iánn)	知(影)	to know	12	110
tsa̍p	十	ten	16	142
tsáu	走	to run; to leave, to go away; to move around	10	93
tsàu-kha / tû-pâng	灶跤 / 廚房	kitchen	19	167
tsáu-lōo	走路	to run away (from creditors, etc); to be on the run	10	93
tsē	坐	to sit; to take (plane, bus, taxi, etc.)	2	33
tsē (S) / tsuē (N)	濟	many, much, plenty	2	33
tsē hui-ki	坐 飛機	to take a plane	2	33
tse-tse / tse--tse	姊姊 / 姊姊	little sister, younger sister (new)	7	71
tshá	吵	noisy; to make a noise, to quarrel, to bother	18	158
tshàu	臭	stinky, smelly	17	151
tshàu-sng	臭酸	to spoil (food), to go/turn sour	17	151
Tsheh tsin kāu	冊 真 厚	The book is really thick.	18	158
tshénn (S) / tshínn (N)	醒	to become awake or sober; to regain consciousness	18	161
tshī	飼	to feed, to raise (animal, child)	4	48
tshī kiánn / tshī gín-á	飼 囝 / 飼 囡仔	to raise children	4	48

INDEX

WORD	漢字	ENGLISH	LESSON	PAGE
tshī-tiûnn	市場	market	5	54
tshia-tsām / tshia-thâu	車站 / 車頭	station	16	141
tshiah-phòng-se	刺膨紗	to knit (with yarn)	8	78
tshiánn	請	please; to host, to treat, to offer someone food and drink	7	70
tshiánn-mn̄g	請問	May I ask...; Could you please tell me... (a polite expression to start a question)	7	70
tshiánn-tsē	請坐	Please take a seat.	7	70
tshīng	穿	to wear, to put on	8	79
tshit	七	seven	14	125
tshit-gue̍h-puànn (S) / tshit-ge̍h-puànn (N)	七月半	The Ghost Festival (The 15th day of the 7th month on the traditional calendar; also known as "Tiong-guân" 中元)	14	125
tshiū-á	樹仔	tree	11	102
tshiū-á-kha	樹仔跤	under the tree	11	103
tshiú-khuân	手環	bracelet	12	110
tshiú-ki-á	手機仔	cell phone, mobile phone	13	119
tshiū-nâ	樹林	woods, forest	11	102
tshiú-tsí	手指	ring	12	110
tshiùnn	唱	to sing	11	102
tshiùnn-kua	唱歌	to sing a song; singing	11	102
tshù	厝	house	4	47
tshù--lí (S) / tshù--nih (N)	厝裡	in the house; at home	4	47
tshù-kak-tsiáu (S) / tshik-tsiáu-á (N)	厝角鳥 / 粟鳥仔	house sparrow	11	102
tshù-lāi	厝內	inside the house; at home; one's household	4	47
tshù-pinn	厝邊	neighbor; neighborhood	2, 4	32, 47
tshù-tíng	厝頂	roof	4	47
tshuē (S) / tshē (N)	揣	to search, to look for	17	150

WORD	漢字	ENGLISH	LESSON	PAGE
tshuē--tio̍h (S) / tshē--tio̍h (N)	揣著	to find	17	150
tshuē-bô (S) / tshē-bô (N)	揣無	didn't find, couldn't find	17	150
Tshuē-ū--bô? (S) / Tshē-ū--bô? (N)	揣有無？	Have you found it?	17	150
tshuì	喙	mouth; mouthful; opening	17	149
tshuì-ta	喙焦	to be thirsty	17	149
tshut	出	to exit, to go out; to occur; to publish	19	169
tshut--khì	出去	to get out, to go out; out (directional complement)	9, 19	86, 169
tshut--lâi	出來	to come out; out (directional complement)	19	169
tshut-kok	出國	to go abroad, to leave the country	9	86
tshut-la̍t	出力	to exert oneself; with all one's might	14	127
tshut-mn̂g	出門	to go out, to leave home; to go on a journey	9	86
tshut-sì	出世	to be born	20	176
tsia	遮	here	14	127
tsia--ê	遮的	these; these ones here	14	127
tsiah	隻	(measure word for ships, airplanes and most animals)	2	32
tsiah	才	and then; only then; before finally...; just, only	10	94
tsia̍h	食	to eat; to drink; to take	5	55
tsia̍h àm(-tǹg)	食暗(頓)	to eat dinner	14	127
tsia̍h io̍h-á	食藥仔	to take medicine	5	55
tsia̍h kah tsiok pá	食甲足飽	to get very full from eating (to eat to the extent of feeling very full)	9	86
tsia̍h mih(-kiānn) (S) / tsia̍h mn̍gh(-kiānn) (N)	食物(件)	to eat something, to eat; eating	17	150
tsia̍h puànn-tàu-á	食半晝仔	to eat brunch (new)	14	127
tsia̍h siunn tsē (S) / tsia̍h siunn tsuē (N)	食傷濟	to eat too much	15	134

INDEX

WORD	漢字	ENGLISH	LESSON	PAGE
tsiàh tiong-tàu(-tǹg)	食 中晝 (頓)	to eat lunch	14	127
tsiàh tsái-khí(-tǹg)	食 早起 (頓)	to eat breakfast	14	127
tsiàh-hun	食薰	to smoke	5	55
tsiàh-la̍t	食力	tough, demanding; serious (sickness or injury)	14	127
tsiàh-pá	食飽	to be full (after having eaten)	5	55
tsiàh-pn̄g	食飯	to have a meal; to eat rice	5	55
tsiah(-nī)	遮 (爾)	so, such (like this)	14	127
tsiânn	誠	so, very	1	25
tsiáu-á	鳥仔	bird	11	102
tsiàu-kòo	照顧	care; to take care of, to look after	13	118
tsin	真	really, truly, very	1	25
Tsin hāi!	真 害！	Goodness! What a mess!	18	159
tsìn-tsîng	進前	before; previously	12	109
Tsîng-jîn-tsiat / Tsîng-jîn-tseh	情人節	Valentine's Day	8	77
tsing-sîn	精神	spirit, mind, energy; to wake up (from sleep)	18	161
tsînn	錢	money	15	135
tsió	少	few, little, less	2	33
tsio-kóo-lè-toh	(チョコレート)	chocolate	20	176
tsio̍h-thâu	石頭	stone, rock	12	110
tsiok / tsok	足	so, very	1	25
tsit	這	this + noun	6	64
tsit	一	one	2	32
tsit ê	一个	one, a	2	32
tsit ê / tse	這个 / 這	this (one), this thing	6	64
tsit kha tshiú-tsí	一跤 手指	a ring ("kha": measure word for rings, boxes, suitcases)	12	110

SHORT TAKES

WORD	漢字	ENGLISH	LESSON	PAGE
tsit ki hōo-suànn	一枝雨傘	an umbrella ("ki": measure word for long items that can be held in hand such as pencils, forks, umbrellas)	9	**86**
tsit ki tshiú-ki-á	一支手機仔	a cell phone ("ki": measure word for phone, nose, mouth, teeth)	13	**119**
tsit king tshù	一間厝	a house ("king" is the measure word for rooms, houses, schools, stores, etc.)	4	**47**
tsit lé-pài	一禮拜	one week	6	**61**
tsit lé-pài tshit kang	一禮拜七工	seven days a week	14	**125**
tsit lia̍p kiû	一粒球	a ball ("liap": measure word for roundish objects or granules such as balls, oranges, stones, pills and grains)	14	**126**
tsit niá khòo	一領褲	a pair of pants	8	**78**
tsit niá kûn	一領裙	a skirt	8	**78**
tsit niá sann	一領衫	a piece of clothing	8	**78**
tsit pha tiān-hué (S) / tsit pha tiān-hé (N)	一葩電火	a light, a lamp ("pha": measure word for lamps, a bunch of flowers, a bunch of grapes)	19	**167**
tsit siang tī	一雙箸	a pair of chopsticks	15	**133**
tsit su sann	一軀衫	a set of clothes, a complete outfit	8	**78**
tsit tâi tiān-náu	一台電腦	a computer ("tâi": measure word for cars, machines and electronic devices)	13	**119**
tsit tiám	一點	one o'clock	10	**94**
tsit tiám-tsing	一點鐘	one hour	10	**94**
tsit tiâu kua	一條歌	a song ("tiâu": measure word for streets, rivers, rope, thread, songs)	11	**102**
tsit tiunn phue	一張批	a letter	3	**41**
tsit tiunn siòng-phìnn	一張相片	a photo ("tiunn": measure word for paper, letters, photos)	7	**69**

INDEX

WORD	漢字	ENGLISH	LESSON	PAGE
tsit tòng lâu	一棟樓	a multi-story building ("tòng": measure word for buildings)	4	48
tsit tsâng tshiū-á	一欉樹仔	a tree ("tsâng": measure word for trees, shrubs, plants)	11	102
tsit tshut tiān-iánn	一齣電影	a/one movie ("tshut": measure word for movies, dramas and plays)	6	62
tsit-kuá / kuá	一寡	some, a few	20	176
tsit-má	這馬	now	1	25
tsit-puànn	一半	a half, one half	17	149
tsit-sì-lâng	這世人	this life, this lifetime	20	176
tsit-sì-lâng	一世人	a lifetime; all one's life	20	176
Tsiú tsiok kāu.	酒足厚。	The liquor is very strong.	18	158
tsò (S) / tsuè (N)	做	to do, to make, to serve/act as	12	109
tsò-hué (S) / tsuè-hué (N)	做伙	together, jointly; to get along, to be together	11	104
tsò-senn-jit (S) / tsuè-sinn-lit (N)	做生日	to celebrate one's birthday; to give a birthday party	12	109
tsò-sing-lí (S) / tsuè-sing-lí (N)	做生理	to do/run a business	8	77
tsóh--jit (S) / tsóh--lit (N)	昨日	the day before yesterday	12	109
tsù-ì	注意	to pay attention, to notice; carefully, closely	13	118
tsuè-kīn (S) / tsuè-kūn (N)	最近	lately, recently	6	63
tú-tsiah / tú-á	拄才 / 拄仔	just now, just a moment ago	13	117
tú(-á)-hó	拄(仔)好	just (in time), just right; it just so happens that...	13	117
tuà	蹛	to live (in), to stay at	2	32
tuā	大	big, large, huge; to grow up	8	79
tuà tī	蹛佇	to live in, at, on	2	32
tuā-hàn	大漢	big and tall (body); the older (birth order); to grow up	8	79
tuā-lâng	大人	adult	8	79

WORD	漢字	ENGLISH	LESSON	PAGE
tuā-sè (S) / tuā-suè (N)	大細	large and small; old and young	8	79
tuā-siann	大聲	loud; to speak loudly or rudely	8	79
tuì / uì	對	from; to, towards, facing; as to, with regard to	16	141
ū	有	to have, to exist; to have/did + verb	2, 6	32, 62
ū tsînn thang bé (S) / ū tsînn thang bué (N)	有錢通買	to have the money to buy	16	143
ū tsînn--bô?	有錢無?	(Do you) have money?	6	62
ū tsit kang	有一工	(there's) one day	6	64
ū-iánn	有影	true, real, genuine; truly, really, genuinely	13	118
ū-iánn--bô?	有影無?	Is it true?	6	62
ū-iánn--ooh	有影喔	Oh, really?	13	118
ū-îng	有閒	to be free, available; to have time	6	61
ū-îng--bô?	有閒無?	(Are you) free? (Do you) have time?	6	62
ū-kàu	有夠	so, extremely, terribly; to be enough	10	93
ū-la̍t	有力	strong, powerful	14	127
ū-sî(-á)	有時(仔)	sometimes	20	176
uánn	碗	bowl (of)	5	56
uē	話	spoken words, speech, language	3	39
uī	位	place, space, position, seat; measure word for persons (formal)	10	94
uī-siánn-mih	為啥物	for what reason, why (new)	14	127
ūn-tōng	運動	to exercise; sports	14	126

www.ingramcontent.com/pod-product-compliance
Lightning Source LLC
Chambersburg PA
CBHW060458010526
44118CB00018B/2460